"*The Chaos Parallel* takes us on a journey into understanding how our insecurities play such a critical role in keeping us from experiencing what is real, even though it seems real at the time. Alex says: 'Our habitual failure to recognize our insecurities and the power they have over us leads to the inevitable consequence of altering our authentic lives.'

"Be encouraged as Alex shares his story and, through it, moves us toward authentic living. Whether in work, marriage, or family life, *The Chaos Parallel* will reveal some unsettling things about you. But in the end, it will help you discover the real you.

"Alex, thank you for taking us on a critical journey in helping us to ask the 'why' in our insecurities that will begin the process of real freedom. The freedom to not only be—but know—who we really are!"

—Dave Dravecky

Retired MLB Pitcher, the San Francisco Giants
Author and Motivational Speaker

"In *The Chaos Parallel*, Alex Geesbreght achieves for business psychology what Daniel Kahneman achieved for behavioral economics—he presents a highly complex and sometimes uncomfortable subject in a digestible and highly entertaining and personal format. This book is a must for any entrepreneur who wants to drive themselves and their organization to the next level."

—Carson Yost, CFA

CEO, Yost Capital Management, L.P.

"A powerful, life-changing book that everyone needs to read. As a professional athlete and entrepreneur, I always feel the pressure of being under the microscope of public opinion, which can magnify even the smallest of insecurities. In *The Chaos Parallel*, Alex invites us to have a conversation with ourselves about ourselves, our decisions, why we do what we do, and how our insecurities can impact every area of our life. His comedic—yet authentic—life story and thought-provoking personal discovery will challenge and encourage you at any stage of life."

—Kevin Conway

NASCAR Cup Series Rookie of the Year
FIA Lamborghini World Champion
Cofounder, PHOOZY

"Alex Geesbreght's book examines how we all get derailed by unexpected or wrong turns in our lives. As I was reading, I could not stop thinking of the many times my kids asked 'Why?' and deserved more than the trite answer I gave them."

—Barclay Berdan

CEO, Texas Health Resources

"To lead successfully at any level requires leaders that are not fooled or misled by their emotions or the emotive behavior of others. In *The Chaos Parallel*, Geesbreght makes the case that before one can fully master their craft, one must first master oneself. To do that requires a deeper understanding of the human element, the ability to listen with the intent to understand—not simply respond. In this seminal work, Geesbreght instructs the reader how to understand why things are happening versus what is happening and how to follow the why to the root cause of any problem. Avoid focusing on the symptoms that mislead and often become the ubiquitous target of resolve. Take your EQ to the next level with this treatise that confirms the notion that success in business, as in life, often comes first from knowing the right questions to ask."

—Ralph W. Manning

CEO and Cofounder, Coltala Holdings
YPO Chapter Chair

THE CHAOS PARALLEL

HOW TO OVERCOME
THE LIFE-ALTERING EFFECTS
OF INSECURITIES

THE
CHAOS
PARALLEL

J. ALEXANDER GEESBREGHT

ForbesBooks

152,46
GEESBREGHT

Published by ForbesBooks, Charleston, South Carolina.
Member of Advantage Media Group.

ForbesBooks is a registered trademark, and the ForbesBooks colophon is a trademark of Forbes Media, LLC.

Printed in the United States of America.

10 9 8 7 6 5 4 3 2 1

ISBN: 978-1-950863-06-8
LCCN: 2019905839

Cover design by Melanie Cloth.
Layout design by Megan Elger.

This publication is designed to provide accurate and authoritative information in regard to the subject matter covered. It is sold with the understanding that the publisher is not engaged in rendering legal, accounting, or other professional services. If legal advice or other expert assistance is required, the services of a competent professional person should be sought.

 Advantage Media Group is proud to be a part of the Tree Neutral® program. Tree Neutral offsets the number of trees consumed in the production and printing of this book by taking proactive steps such as planting trees in direct proportion to the number of trees used to print books. To learn more about Tree Neutral, please visit **www.treeneutral.com**.

Since 1917, the Forbes mission has remained constant. Global Champions of Entrepreneurial Capitalism. ForbesBooks exists to further that aim by bringing the Stories, Passion, and Knowledge of top thought leaders to the forefront. ForbesBooks brings you The Best in Business. To be considered for publication, please visit **www.forbesbooks.com**.

For Smooge, Yo-Yo, and Bibby

TABLE OF CONTENTS

FOREWORD

I don't remember the first time I met Alex, but I know he remembers meeting me. Mom and Dad introduced us as big brother and little sister—a relationship that would forever shape my life.

From the beginning, I found myself looking up to him. At first, it was our obvious height difference, but then it became adoration, an inside joke, an alliance. I've seen him win baseball games, learn to play guitar, drive a stick shift, and lose baseball games. I've witnessed him walk across the stage at graduations, get pulled over and repeatedly let off the hook, and ski down the first hole of a golf course (that one time it snowed in Texas). I've watched him become a lawyer, a husband, a father, a business owner, and now an author. Over the past year, I've had the privilege of sitting across from Alex at bustling coffee shops and on breezy terraces in LA, listening to him read portions of this book, which I instantly recognized as being a combination of my brother's brain and heart. It struck me. He's always been writing this book. Every loss and every triumph were bricks laid in the path to the pages ahead.

I am a songwriter. I've been stringing words together with melodies since I can remember. I get to sit in rooms in Nashville, Tennessee, across from recording artists and write three-minute stories. I've seen music careers ebb and flow, crash and burn, and rise and thrive. I, too, have ridden that roller coaster. But I've found the thing that gives anyone working in the music industry relevance and longevity is authenticity. It's what produces those few hits among a thousand misses. Isn't it true that the songs that resonate with us are the ones that have heart—the ones where you feel the cohesion between the person singing and the message in the song? If we see or hear a disconnect—even for a moment—we tend to do the same and move on.

As long as I can remember, Alex has been able to connect the person with the message. He is an engaging conversationalist and an excellent asker of questions—like the really good ones. The ones that challenge your perception of your reality, spur self-awareness, and demand an authentic and honest response. With natural charm and quick wit, he softens the moment. You will experience this "voice" and find yourself craving its tone. Alex's fluid introspection and fresh, "telling it like it is" attitude is contagious.

When I'm in co-write with someone new, we'll usually start with a few foundational questions: "How are you?"; "Where are you from?"; "When did you get into music?" But what kind of song would we write if we stopped there? How compelling would the lyrics be if this were as deep as we went? Imagine if we only experienced the "what" (wrote a song) and never acknowledged one of the many "whys" (said something honest). It might sound basic and even obvious, but how often do we take our relationships, our jobs, or our parenting and ask "Why?"

In the pages ahead, if you choose to read them, you will undoubtedly begin to recognize your Chaos Parallel and how to move closer to the life you were intended to live. However, this book is not for the faint of heart. You will be invited to take an uncomfortable look at your insecurities and will begin to notice those in the people around you. If you are accustomed to blaming others for all your problems—or know those who are—your instinct may be to put this book down. Don't. Prepare yourself not just for the song, but for something honest.

—April Geesbreght Cushman

ACKNOWLEDGMENTS

Due to the nature of this book, I must acknowledge life, in general. Every person I have met—each conversation, disagreement, and relationship—has had an impact on me and the words in this book.

Specifically, I want and need to first acknowledge He who is most important. Without Him, nothing in my life would be possible or worthwhile. Throughout the book I reference or allude to "hope"— that promise of tomorrow. It is the thing that drives all of us and keeps us going when the going gets tough. In a world full of relativism and ever-changing societal norms, God is a constant. He is the eternal source of my hope.

As for the specific people who helped me on this journey, they are too numerous to name. This might be a blessing in disguise, as many of my life lessons—which are the basis of this book—have come from observing, interacting with, and knowing people who were excellent examples of what not to do. I doubt they would like to be "acknowledged" for their contribution.

But there are scores of people who have served as friends, mentors, and confidants as it relates to this book and my life, in general. They were sounding boards and constant cheerleaders as I embarked on this endeavor. They convincingly feigned interest as they listened intently while I read them the tenth version of the sixth paragraph of chapter three. A thousand thank-yous to each of you. I also wish to thank my editor, Tiara, who saw the vision for this book immediately and was inspirational and encouraging throughout. And I want to thank all of the great people at Advantage|ForbesBooks. The patience each of you showed toward this first-time author was remarkable.

There is one person, in particular, who I would like to highlight; someone, for whatever reason, I never mention in the book, but without whom my life as I know it would not exist. In a family of large personalities and attention seekers, she has always been content to appear to take a back seat. The reality is, however, we all know who is driving us forward. We've always known. Priscilla Geesbreght is my mom (technically, she is my "step-mom"). She has raised me as her own since I was four years old.

The wonderful mom I refer to in this book is my biological mom, Mary Lee, for whom I also have great love, respect, and admiration. My words here do nothing to take away from the gratitude and understanding I have for her life and the tremendous impact she has on mine, as my "mom in Chicago." I have learned to love both of them equally, if not somewhat differently. The zero-sum game I thought I needed to play as a child has been replaced with an adult understanding of just how insanely fortunate I am to have them both—that it is okay to love them both. My moms.

In the book, I write about and reference my mom and dad, a sibling or two, my wife, kids, friends, etc. and how they each impacted my life, thoughts, feelings, and actions. But it is my strong belief that the cornerstone of my life is not any of them. It is my mom, Priscilla. She was not the never-ending source of wisdom that my dad was, nor did we ever share the unbreakable, inextricable link that I have with my mom, Mary Lee. She wasn't uber-inspirational like my kids are, nor would it be fair to compare her to what my wife, Carey, has meant to me.

What she was—and is—in many ways, was far more important to the course and direction of my life. She was there. She was solid. She was constant. She was loving. She was patient. She was all of those things and a hundred more, and remains so to this day.

How does one undo the ringing of a bell? How does one envision—or feel—a life without the stability she provided? I will thankfully never know the answer to that question, because of her.

As a quiet, twenty-four-year-old daughter of a preacher, her first interaction with me was when she walked in our house only to be greeted by a chubby three-year-old with a mop of red hair, screeching at the top of his lungs that he was Superman, as he wore the pajamas that proved it.

She should have turned around right then. But she didn't. She stayed—to my great and everlasting benefit.

ABOUT THE AUTHOR

Alex Geesbreght is the founder and partner of Geesbreght Group, L.P. He is a graduate of Texas Christian University, where he received his degree in radio, television, and film. He later received his JD from the University of Tulsa College of Law. In his early career, Alex was a civil litigator specializing in medical malpractice defense, and later served as a Tarrant County assistant district attorney. Alex is a former owner of Emergency Medicine Consultants, where he served for over sixteen years in various roles, including as general counsel, president, and chief strategy officer, until the sale of the company in 2018. Alex is also the former owner and CEO of PhysAssist Scribes, the nation's first medical scribe company. While growing PhysAssist, Alex was selected as a finalist for the Ernst & Young Entrepreneur of the Year Award. Since selling PhysAssist in 2014, Alex has become a full-time investor and counselor of early stage entrepreneurs. He is heavily involved in the Young Presidents' Organization (YPO) where he sits on the board of directors for the Fort Worth Chapter and is currently the education chair. Alex serves as the chairman of Friends of Southwest on behalf of Texas Health Southwest hospital. He lives in Fort Worth, Texas, with his wife, Carey, their three children

(John, Joe, and Vivian), and their five rescue dogs (Henri, Louie, Sneaky, Lucy, and Tucker).

OUR SERVICES

Geesbreght Group, L.P., is an investment and leadership consulting firm that offers equity/debt financing, strategic management solutions, and executive coaching to small businesses. Founded by Alex Geesbreght, the group believes that success is defined by *doing what you love, with those whom you love*. With a dynamic blend of passion and skill, their focus is helping entrepreneurs and leaders create, define, and execute their goals. The group targets partnerships with early businesses seeking capital, strategic guidance, and leadership training to scale and maximize profit and organizational stability.

HAVE YOU EVER SEEN *THE THING BEHIND THE THING?*

I am dying. I'm almost forty-five years old, and based on everything they know, the doctors say I may only have between thirty-five and forty years left.

Don't feel sorry for me, though. It's been a good run. Thus far, I've lived a life full of love, sadness, adventure, success, and failure. Well, now that I put it that way, perhaps it hasn't been that great; it basically sounds like everyone else's life. So, here is my chance to change that.

This is my attempt at seizing the opportunity to do what I enjoy most—while I still have time. Even with all I've experienced in these forty-five years, nothing has ever made me happier than making a lasting, meaningful impact on the lives around me. Hopefully this book will help me continue my mission.

That mission has since inspired me to combine my greatest passions with a few hard lessons and, somehow, I produced a book in the process. I live this message every day. I eagerly share it with whomever I believe will benefit from it. My wife, my children, my friends, my business associates, my neighbors—they've all been briefed on the omnipresent interference that is "insecurity"—the often-silent, but wholly disruptive, companion to us all.

I advocate for all to identify the "*The Thing Behind the Thing*"— the root cause or motivation of what is in front of us—hiding somewhere within all our human interactions. This book was designed as a guide to help first identify, then overcome, its hold—if that's the road you choose.

The words on these pages come directly from my heart. I share my story in hopes that you will be able to recognize congruencies that align with your own. While standing on that common ground, I believe we can begin to collectively raise the veil on a life-altering parallel and overcome the effects of our insecurities as we search for the *The Thing Behind the Thing* together.

The Chaos Parallel—a portion of your life based on your reactions to insecurities that runs parallel to, but different from, your intended life.

EXPLORING THE EFFECTS OF INSECURITY

In the following chapters, you'll recognize two overarching concepts. The first offers a formal introduction to the gateway that guards *The Thing Behind the Thing*, in all its multifarious manifestations. This discovery will welcome you to something I like to call the Chaos Parallel.

We will spend some time examining the role insecurities play in our lives before moving on to the next concept: recognizing how *The Thing Behind the Thing* can be incredibly valuable. On rare occasions, insecurities, such as fear of the embarrassment that comes from failure, can have a motivating, and thus positive, effect. But in the vast majority of cases, our insecurities keep us from ourselves—masking all manner of our real thoughts, feelings, words, or actions; they separate us from our most authentic selves.

Insecurity is often responsible for the deterioration, or outright destruction, of many of our relationships with family, friends, and coworkers. But perhaps the most damaged relationship of all is the one we have with ourselves—the way we view and value our own lives, especially from behind the veil.

Our habitual failure to recognize our insecurities and the power they have over us leads to the inevitable consequence of altering our authentic lives. It's amazing to see how the subtlest action (or inaction) can send us rushing down a path that is closely related to, but altogether different from, the life we intended to live. What's even more amazing is that most don't ever recognize the signs and symptoms of the Chaos Parallel—at least, not before enduring a few of the unapologetic lessons its musings teach us.

For the purposes of this book, it is important that you have not so much of a working definition, but rather, a working *understanding* of what the Chaos Parallel is. It is my sincere hope that you will become able to recognize it, remove yourself from it, and, eventually, avoid it altogether.

Have you ever taken a step back from the chaos your life has devolved into and asked, "How did I get here?" Now, imagine if that question wasn't rhetorical. Suppose the answer mattered.

What if you could actually trace your steps back to the very moment in time when your life, your current state, or a simple conversation got off track? Take a minute to really think about that. The fact is, you absolutely can. In doing so, you'll find your way straight to *The Thing Behind the Thing*, while gaining clarity and insight into the root cause of your present circumstance.

WHAT IS THE CHAOS PARALLEL?

I want you to imagine that you are driving your car on your way to meet a friend for dinner. Somewhere along the way, you take a wrong turn. That wrong turn is followed by another, then another, with each wrong turn being the predictable result of the last, and more than a contributing factor in the next. By the end of the evening, instead of enjoying what was sure to be a lovely dinner with your friend, you wake up in a seedy motel room with a flashing neon vacancy sign surrounded by three hookers and a man named Billy Bob asking who you work for. Don't laugh, this happened to me. Okay, it didn't, and the example is absurd, but I use it to make the point. You don't know *how* you got there, but you should recognize *why*. You took a wrong turn.

"I don't need help. I've got this," you convinced yourself. Instead of following the directions your friend texted you, your ego got in the way and you decided to use your Magellan-like powers to go at it alone. Your insecurity caused you to take the wrong turn, and the turn itself led to the chaos your life became in that moment. Your current reality—everything you had to live through and all the things you were forced to see inside that god-awful Roach Motel—is the Chaos Parallel, not the life—or the evening—you intended.

For now, just think of the Chaos Parallel as a segment of time that is playing out due to false pretenses. If you have ever found yourself in a fight with a spouse, significant other, friend, or colleague based on something that had nothing to do with the actual subject matter of the fight itself, you have lived at least a portion of your life in the Chaos Parallel. The impact this parallel course has on all aspects of our lives can be short-lived or lifelong, and can range from the benign to the totally catastrophic.

The second and more all-encompassing concept this book explores is the value of looking for and recognizing *The Thing Behind the Thing*—searching for and understanding the "why," or the root cause, in everything. While insecurity is perhaps the most glaring and damaging example of a thing behind a thing, it is but one. In fact, the backdrop, motivation, and context for this entire book is predicated on the importance of looking beyond what is in front of us, and asking and understanding why.

> **Recognizing *The Thing Behind the Thing*—searching for and understanding the "why," or the root cause, in everything.**

Doing so gives life layers, depth, and context. With that comes awareness, understanding, and in many cases, peace of mind.

An inextricable part of the two main concepts in this book is the tremendous value of seeing the world as it is, not as we wish it were, so we can begin building trust through effective communication, authenticity, and vulnerability. If you watch a tenth of the amount of television I do, you know that advertisers believe we have an insatiable appetite for things that are real. The promise of authenticity is everywhere as an aspirational trait to be valued and purchased. Yet, the reason it is treasured is because it remains so rare in our everyday lives.

Why do we crave "real"? Why do we constantly issue the compliment of a person we admire by describing them as "so down to earth" and "authentic"? We admire these traits in others because we expect less of them and perhaps ourselves. Why is that, really?

Why do we wear expensive suits and layers of makeup during the day, only to reveal our T-shirts and washed, natural faces to those few trusted souls awaiting us at home and out of view from the rest of the world? What are we afraid of? Why are we afraid?

I'm not suggesting that we don't get dressed up for work, or church, or our kids' recitals; what I'm asking is, when did authenticity become a commodity and how can we begin to normalize it again?

Although I am prepared to close this introduction with those weighted questions floating in the air, I plan to satiate your appetite for answers in the coming pages. But, before I turn you loose, here is my final disclaimer. You don't know me (yet). You don't yet know that I see each conversation I have, each speech I give, and yes, each chapter I write from about thirty thousand feet in the air. I can assure you that, while you read, there will be moments where you will swear that I have started writing another book entirely. All I can tell you is that I haven't. The detours are intentional, and they have purpose. Stick with it, *please*. My promise to you is that you can take the journey off the path with the knowledge and confidence that you will find your way back safely.

I hope you enjoy it.

CHAPTER ONE

LIFTING THE MASK

T hroughout human history, you'll find many instances of seemingly instinctive nonverbal cues that tend to have a somewhat interesting backstory. One such example can be found in the history of the military salute. It is said that saluting began in France, where knights would lift their metal mask or visor when meeting others to reveal their eyes—or as some believe, the window to our souls.

The practice served to build and gain trust by revealing the vulnerability that comes with identification and known intention.[1] The same is true today. When we show others who we really are, we let them in. And, if billions of dollars of marketing research are any indication, being real is something to be desired, admired, and sought after.

---

1   "The Stories Behind the Modern Military Salute," USO, July 9, 2015, https://www.uso.org/stories/1646-the-stories-behind-the-modern-military-salute.

We tend to hold those who dare to unmask themselves as comfortable and confident, as perhaps people worth emulating and following. In other words, these are the people we trust to become leaders. Whether we are leading our employees, friends, or children, wear a suit when necessary, but be mindful of the value in taking off your mask. It's good for them to see you in a T-shirt occasionally.

Revealing yourself to others often requires you to first be comfortable and secure with who you are. To achieve this, you must first know who you are, which is usually gained through experience and introspection. One of the best pieces of advice I ever got from my dad was to never wear your job like a pair of pants. He must have said this to us kids a million times, beginning before we were even old enough to have a lemonade stand. He was insistent that we knew who we were, what we were passionate about, and that we chose professions we didn't have to "put on" in the morning. In other words, our job should be a natural extension of the person we were, not what we did. He promised—which proved to be true, like so much of his advice to me—that if we followed this simple rule, we would never work a day in our lives.

ASK THE QUESTION: WHO AM I?

My dad's words began a lifelong obsession within me, inspiring me to find out who I am and to recognize who others are, despite their game attempts to hide it.

When I was a senior in high school, our yearbook afforded each senior his or her own page at the back. The page consisted of a senior photo (mine was with my dog, Kyoto), a couple paragraphs of nonsensical inside jokes put there by classmates, and then a quote. Seniors got to pick their own quote. We could use the words of someone famous, some inspirational adage, or, as I decided, we could simply make one up. Beneath my senior picture read the words, "Be what you want others to become." I don't recall exactly why I wrote that or what I was thinking when I did. What I do know is that I went twenty-plus years without so much as consciously thinking of it. Then, a couple years ago, I was lecturing one of my kids, and I said, "Be what you want others to become." That moment sparked an instant revelation. It caused me to realize that I had lived, or at least attempted to live, my senior quote.

After my interaction with my child brought these words to life, I thought about the years I spent in my business and how I interacted with my employees, friends, and family throughout my life. For the first time, I sat down to reflect on what I could have meant by what now appeared to be a self-fulfilling prophecy. What did I want to be that was so important for others to become? What would your answer be if I asked you the same question?

This book is intended to shine a bright light on insecurity—an ever-present, if not uncomfortable, part of our humanity—and how it plagues our condition. The real-world observations and stories in this book are the culmination of my nearly thirty-year fascination with the negative effects of insecurity and what appears to be our universal refusal to examine or search for the root cause of those effects.

> **This book is intended to shine a bright light on insecurity—an ever-present, if not uncomfortable, part of our humanity—and how it plagues our condition.**

These chapters eschew the perceived value of knowing what happened, but instead focus on the overwhelming importance of asking, "Why?" Essentially, this book is intended to force you to begin looking beyond the "thing" that is the issue or conflict at hand, and learn to appreciate the value of examining and understanding *The Thing Behind the Thing*. I want you to look at the actions, thoughts, and words of others (and yourself) through the prism of "why" and learn to recognize the signs and symptoms of a life altered by insecurities.

For example, if I stub my toe and shout an expletive, the word I scream is the "thing," but the pain or embarrassment I feel is what I should be focused on, because it is the thing that *caused* the thing. While this is an overly simplistic example, here is why the distinction is important: If someone were to walk in the room and only hear me screaming a cuss word, they would form an opinion right then and there. Regardless of what that opinion was, the one certainty is that it would differ from the one they would have formed had they seen what caused me to scream.

The Thing Behind the Thing is the often-indiscernible cause of the "what" appearing in front of us. In our never-ending quest to process information, we often gravitate toward the most obvious or expedient explanation. We rather reflexively convince ourselves that there is no need to look further. However, as in the aforementioned example, many of our conclusions are based on incomplete information. Also consider that much of the information we consume is specifically intended to mislead—or at least distract (think of just about any advertisement). Train yourself to instinctively look beyond the shiny object and question. Doing so is a necessary component of learning from and making sense of the people and circumstances around us. We will discuss how this practice and learned skill can be one of life's most comforting and powerful tools.

LIFTING MY MASK: WHAT CAUSED MY WHY?

While the vast majority of this book explores all things "why," it would be foolish of me to hide the "what" from you. Now, I'm no knight in shining armor, but consider this to be me briefly lifting my metal visor. Because, as with all books—especially this one—positioning, context, and perspective matter. If you watch any movie or TV show, you will notice what is called an "establishing shot" at the beginning of nearly every scene. It is intended to provide the viewer with a frame of reference. Since so much of what is to come is told through the lens of my experiences, it is worth briefly noting "what" I am.

What I am is extremely fortunate. I was born lucky—a truth I fought for years, attempting instead to convince myself and others that my success was the direct and sole result of my hard work. Don't get me wrong, I work hard, but lots of people work hard, harder than I do. To pretend that we all start from the same place is absurd. The older I got, the more I realized that selling that narrative to myself and others was like trying to turn a square into a circle. The inherent and obvious incongruence built nothing but insecurity and guilt.

I grew up hearing the story of the kid who was born on third base and thought he had hit a triple. I was determined to not be that kid. What I eventually realized was that I couldn't do anything about the base I was born on; feeling guilty about it was pointless and counterproductive. What I could do was be grateful, work like hell to justify all I had, and fight to get to home so I could score on my own.

Now, here's why I would call myself lucky.

I grew up in Fort Worth, Texas, with a family who loved and supported me. Even childhood challenges, like my parents' divorce, were somehow turned into lifelong lessons that exposed me to positive influences and experiences I would not have otherwise had. I impulsively attended law school after college, and practiced both civil and criminal litigation for a few years before joining my dad's healthcare company as its general counsel. But it wasn't until I grew my own company that I was free to test who I was, and what I wanted others to become.

My company, PhysAssist Scribes, afforded me the opportunity to build something, but more importantly, to help build others and to be a force for good in their professional and personal lives. During that decade of my professional career, we enjoyed some phenomenal successes. PhysAssist helped revolutionize the process through which physicians and other healthcare providers delivered care by freeing them from the strains and drains of documenting their work on the then newly mandated Electronic Medical Record, or EMR. We gave thousands and thousands of pre-medical students a job that helped prepare them for a career in medicine. Equally important, we served as a filter for those who quickly learned that a life in medicine was not for them.

PhysAssist, as a startup, was also the first corporate job for many who would become our corporate executives. They cut their teeth at PhysAssist. Having young and inexperienced executives is not unusual for a startup company. What is extremely unusual is that nearly all of them are still with the company today.

Over those ten years, we were on numerous "fastest growing company" lists and the focus of countless national articles, and I was selected as a finalist for the Ernst & Young Entrepreneur of the Year award, which was much more about my team than it was about me. That's not false humility; it's a fact. I just happened to be the guy at the top of the organizational chart.

Ultimately, in 2014, I sold the company to a longtime client and strategic partner, TeamHealth. PhysAssist Scribes had simply grown too big for me to continue connecting with people the way I felt was meaningful and in line with my skill set. Despite my waning interest, it was a difficult decision to make. I was aware of the fact that I would be forever forfeiting the right to command the direction of the company, thus serving and protecting my employees. In late 2018, I felt the effect of my decision. After owning PhysAssist for less than four years, TeamHealth sold it to our longtime competitor, ScribeAmerica. Initially, the news was a tough pill to swallow. However, I take great comfort in the fact that my former company and its people are back in the hands of those who understand and appreciate their value.

In any event, while many in this world measure my success by the number associated with the sale of my company, I measure success quite differently and always have. I use my own scorecard. First, I have a drawer full of notes, letters, and emails I collected over the years from employees and even former employees who mostly never mention their professional interactions with me. Rather, in those notes, letters, and emails, they say back to me much of what I spent ten years telling them. The fact that they listened is my reward, and the fact that I had a meaningful impact on their lives is everything.

Secondly, for years following the sale, I would drive to PhysAssist every few months and walk the halls, as I used to before I sold. For me, success is measured by the looks on the faces of my former employees whenever they see me coming. It's in the hugs I get and the genuine questions of interest, inquiring about how I'm doing now.

And finally, my greatest barometer of success comes from my family. Despite me basically being on the road for a decade during some of the most formative years of my children's lives, there is not a twinge of resentment, but rather quite the opposite. Being physically gone taught me how to be emotionally present when I was home—a lesson that continues to pay dividends with both my wife and my kids.

Are you familiar with the management concept of the Peter Principle? It posits the notion that people tend to be promoted to their level of incompetence. It assumes that a person's success in one role will transfer to a higher one. However, the differences in the skills needed to succeed in the new role are often ignored and the once rising star is hurled back to Earth. These are actually happy endings for everyone involved. The bad story is the one that is currently taking place in one form or another in every business across the globe. All too often, the misplaced leader is left to wallow in his or her misaligned position of authority, leaving scores of frustrated employees to find ways over, around, and through their insecure boss.

This almost happened to me while writing this book. At a few points in the process, my publishers and editor encouraged me to write this book from the perspective of a "successful business leader." I tried. Not only did I try, I wrestled with the idea itself for months. Ultimately, I got up the courage to schedule a difficult phone call, but one I knew I needed to have. I informed them that while it might be reasonable to view me as a business leader, it felt like another attempt to put a square peg in a round hole.

It felt disingenuous. I am not a "business leader"—I never was. What I am, however, is a person who is pretty in tune with my few gifts, and, far more importantly, a person who is well aware of my many shortcomings. I am a person who loves to lead *people*, not employees. In short, I love helping them get the most out of themselves and their relationships and finding the comfort, clarity, and happiness that come with knowing who they are and who they aren't.

While this book may not specifically be about leadership in business, it is, in many ways, about the traits and characteristics of effective leaders and effective *people*. Communication in all its forms, the ability and willingness to be vulnerable at times, the self-awareness that comes from introspection, and the asking of "why" are all concepts that should be understood and practiced. The most important person you will ever lead is yourself. As the flight attendants say, "Put your own mask on first, then help those seated next to you."

Whether based on lessons learned during my career, my own personal struggles, firsthand accounts from those affected by their insecurities, or the countless historic examples, the content ahead is intended to reveal the true cause of the resulting action. While this book makes no attempt to "cure" or "fix" the issues you might face while reading, I hope it provides an explanation for why you are experiencing them, serving as a resource to help combat the negative influence of the Chaos Parallel.

I have found that simply having a place to put these thoughts and feelings can provide comfort and clarity. The journey each of you will embark upon after reading this book is as personal as it is unique. My sincere wish for you is to find these pages thought provoking and encouraging. But mostly, I hope it will help you make sense of the world around you as you look out among others and, most importantly, into yourself.

CHAPTER TWO

WHY?

I've been overweight my entire life. Not like distractingly overweight, but always noticeable. Sure, like most people who struggle with weight, I've had my share of inspired weeks, months, even years. At times, I even managed to get myself into what many would consider good shape. My lack of consistent motivation can likely be attributed to the fact that it never really seemed to affect my physical participation in almost anything. I've always been very active and reasonably athletic—able to continue playing and significantly contribute in my adult soccer, flag football, and baseball leagues. I was fast and quick as a kid despite being heavy—or "husky" as the euphemism goes—and I remain so to this day. I was never picked last, or even close to it, especially by people who had played with me before. Since I never was a particularly good student, I even fancied myself as an "athlete." I believe others did, as well.

But, despite my relative success and consistent pats on the back in this area, I always shied away from certain sports. Okay, I didn't *shy* away from them; I avoided them like the plague.

Swimming—nope.

Basketball—too great a chance of someone saying, "Shirts and Skins!" after we picked teams.

Wrestling—have you seen that singlet? Way too revealing.

Boxing—ha … not a chance.

But what if I had been good at one of them? What if I didn't carefully have to plan my day and schedule meeting places with friends around the avoidance of such activities? Would my life experiences have been different? Lessons? Memories? Friends? Enemies? Where would the differences end?

Would I be different?

Since there isn't much point to asking or answering these rhetorical questions from yesteryear, perhaps these are better questions:

1. Why did I do this?

2. What caused my behavior?

3. What was I afraid of?

4. Was I aware of the underlying reason behind my actions?

5. Am I doing the same thing now?

The point is, my life was altered in an immeasurable way because of the insecurity I had about my weight. But it wasn't even my weight. To pass it off as such would be to miss the point entirely.

The real issue was that I was afraid of what I thought others would think if they saw me with my shirt off.

Digging a bit deeper, one could say it was what others thought about my weight, but even that doesn't capture it. The real issue was that I was afraid of what I thought others would think if they saw me with my shirt off. Mind you, I was the exact same person with or without a shirt. It was not as if the shirt was a magic shield that confused people into thinking I was thin. Logically, I knew that. Looking back, it was not about others; it was about me. *I was The Thing Behind the Thing.*

As a kid, I remember visiting my mom in Chicago in the summertime and riding my bike down to Oak Street Beach on Lake Michigan with my friends. While I made excuses not to get in the lake, my friends played in what I knew had to be exquisitely refreshing water. I remember marveling at any overweight person, especially a kid, who was walking around with his shirt off without a care in the world. I was jealous of him instead of judging him. For the life of me, I could not understand how anyone could do that. How dare he be so authentic? Wasn't he worried? The answer was no. For whatever reason, he did not share my insecurity. And, for whatever reason, I allowed it to keep me trapped inside the Chaos Parallel. And my life was changed because of it.

It's occurring to me, as I sit here, that if I continue to perpetrate this fraud on you via my continued use of the past tense, I will be doing all of us a great disservice. I'm forty-five years old. I have a wife of eighteen years, three amazing children, the exact number of friends I want and more than I deserve, along with a positive outlook on life. I'm blessed beyond all measure. In addition to that, I've enjoyed some professional success and don't spend much time keeping score or comparing myself, or what I have, to others. Of all my faults, I tend not to be burdened by personal or professional relativism, for which I am extremely grateful. However, when it comes to my weight, I am still that twelve-year-old boy standing on the shores of Lake Michigan longing to be set free from my greatest fear.

While it would be easy to blame the last hour of unproductive staring into space on writer's block, between you and me, that just isn't the reason. The fact is that I know what must come next, and I'm not looking forward to it. So, let me stall a bit and set the stage.

As I write these words, I am sitting on a café patio across from the Montage Hotel in Beverly Hills. I have my obligatory coffee, which I haven't touched, to stake my claim as a paying patron deserving of the prime real estate I'm occupying among the beautiful people. My perch is also quite strategically located in the shade, as my pale skin's love-hate relationship with the sun has become increasingly one-sided.

This city is quite the place to be when writing about insecurities, especially those having to do with physical appearance. These people could make Adonis rethink his workout routine—or, at least, who his plastic surgeon is. By the way, this coffee thing, I do it all the time, and not just as a prop. I routinely make and order coffee and never take a sip. My wife, who helps keep Colombian farmers in business, gives me holy hell for it. Why do I do this?

The "why" question. Why anything? Although unlikely, I suppose there is a chance I might later tackle the silly question of why I make and order drinks I have no intention of consuming. But the habit of asking *why* is a good one. It forces us to practice something that is increasingly rare in this headline society in which we live. Too often we stop at the "what," when "why" holds all the answers.

While doing my best to stay away from partisan politics, I believe we have become sadly obsessed with "What happened?" which is followed by the derivative, "How do I feel about what happened?" which is increasingly code for, "How do I feel about what I think or feel happened?" Of course, there are several problems with these habits, but the greatest among them is the total avoidance of the question "Why did it happen?"

I'm not sure if it made the news, but we had a presidential election in 2016 where the presumptive winner did the unimaginable—she didn't win. Despite the obvious conclusion, she went on a months-long tour promoting her book while avoiding the real question as to why. Wouldn't the answer to *that* question be an important one to know for future elections? It doesn't matter what your party affiliation is, both have lost major elections in the past and both will lose them in the future. In a representative democracy, understanding "why" is what allows the party to become more in touch with its would-be constituents.

At the risk of sounding like a broken record, the problem is only partially with the fact that she focused on her book's title, *What Happened.* The more important question, again, is why she focused on the what. Look, it's not a tough question to answer; we can all understand why it would be tough to face, much less talk about losing a presidential election. The hopes and dreams of roughly half the country hinged on her becoming the first female president. The victory was to be as symbolic as it was ideological. Millions and millions of people were deeply hurt by her loss. You don't need to have a bleeding heart to imagine the pressure, the responsibility, and ultimately the disappointment one would feel in that position.

Nevertheless, I would argue that one owes it to those same people to learn from the experience.

As the name at the top of the ticket at the time, the buck stopped with her. She was the boss. Whether in relation to our employees, our children, or ourselves, we are all the boss of someone, and responsibility starts with us. Would stepping out, taking unqualified ownership, and exposing one's campaign choices be deeply painful, humbling, and embarrassing? Yes. Without question. But guess what else it would have been? *Helpful. Revealing. Educational.*

It might have even been cathartic to allow a deeply confused base to heal and make sense of the world they now live in. Focusing on the "what" may shield us from facing our insecurities but understanding *why* moves us forward.

WHY ASK WHY?

Perhaps asking why is difficult because it forces thought, perspective, and the consideration of motives. It requires thinking. What's worse is that it demands open-minded thought, especially when asking such questions of oneself. If done in an authentic manner, it leads to inevitable introspection and the dreaded by-product of same—vulnerability.

Despite being hard, asking *why* is a good habit to get into for several reasons. Since the day my oldest son could conceptualize, I have been telling him to never focus on "the thing." Instead, always examine *The Thing Behind the Thing*. It's always *The Thing Behind the Thing*.

It's not what *is* that is important. It's the root cause that must be understood. It's not that I don't go swimming; it's why I don't. And, it's not that your boss never misses an opportunity to knock you down a few notches; it's why he does. What drives the action or inaction? Asking and, more importantly, understanding the motivation behind some of life's most common human behaviors helps to make sense of the world around us and the people in it. If we are lucky—and honest—it can even help us explain ourselves. And, if we can explain it, in ourselves or in others, then we can change it, or, at the very least, combat it where necessary.

Perhaps the best reason to dig a little deeper is that there are no lessons to be learned in the what—only in the why. The whats in life are singular in nature and as unique as the circumstances that create them. They are easily described, since they simply are or are not. The whys are far more complex and often difficult, even uncomfortable, to explain. However, if objectively examined and thoroughly understood, they serve as predictive tools to be applied to a variety of circumstances. In terms of lessons to be learned—understanding, context, and growth—the whats in life merely serve as the basis from which the whys are born.

I'll explain what I mean, but allow me a brief set-up. Before impulsively deciding to attend law school, the only thing I ever wanted to be in life was a sports broadcaster. During college, I worked all four years as an intern at the local NBC affiliate in Dallas. I wrote for the college paper, hosted three different sports radio shows, all while broadcasting baseball, basketball, and high school football. But the highlight of my broadcasting "career" came in 1994 while I was attending TCU. I was hired—that's right, actual money instead of the experience-as-compensation model—by the now defunct Fort Worth Cavalry of the Arena Football League, as its color analyst. Now, in point of fact, I didn't actually receive a game check, but I did get a per-diem, which I thought was the coolest thing to ever happen to me. And I was not their first choice—probably not by a long shot. But, as the "now defunct" description may have indicated, money was tight and I was cheap.

Further, I didn't even do it for the entire season; I only filled in for four games for the regular color analyst, Todd Davis. The punch line is that I was a color analyst for a professional football team for four glorious games at the age of twenty. And even if my time in a professional broadcast booth was brief and for budgetary reasons, rather than the competence I thought I possessed, as I reflect, I believe it is the only thing that makes me able to use the word "career" in reference to my broadcasting life.

Looking back, of all the sports I ever broadcasted, I never once served as the play-by-play commentator; I was always the color analyst. See, play-by-play, especially on radio, exists to describe for the listener what is taking place that cannot be seen. On television, since the viewer can presumably see the action, the play-by-play commentator serves a slightly more in-depth function of describing not only the X's and O's, but the portions of the game on which he or she believes the viewer should be focused. For instance, the commentator might say:

"The Falcons line up in a single-back formation with trip receivers right. Thompson drops back, avoids the rush, scrabbles right and throws off the wrong foot, but completes the pass for the first down."

There. That happened.

Necessary? Yes.

Informative? Definitely.

Interesting?

Insightful?

I never thought so.

It only described what happened, not why it happened or what made it possible, and, therefore, likely to happen or not happen in the future.

The color analyst, on the other hand, serves a far different purpose from that of the play-by-play commentator. He or she is there to explain the how and the why. Their job is to take the picture of what happened and frame it, so to speak. They are there to paint the backdrop, the landscape, and the other influences that provide depth, context, reason, and meaning to an otherwise self-explanatory picture—hence the name "color" analyst. So, in this case, the color analyst might say, usually at the conclusion of the play:

"Bob, the ability that Thompson has to avoid the rush coming from behind is no accident. His grandfather was a football coach, as well as his dad. Thompson told me before the game that his dad started working with him as a young child on how to sense and avoid pressure in the pocket and turn a busted play into positive yardage."

Now we know something. Something useful. Something we can apply to the future. We now know that the play itself was no fluke. Thompson wasn't just lucky; his actions were intentional. We now know that he possesses the necessary skills through years of training that not only made that play possible, but, more importantly, similar plays in the future possible. The point is that we know something that was not simply observable. Anyone with a TV can see what happened; the reason we watch a game with the sound turned up is to find out why.

Okay, I've stalled long enough, even if for the valid purpose of explaining the importance of "why," which serves as the thematic backdrop for everything else you'll read in this book. So back to present tense. Again, even writing about this is embarrassing, but here's my confession:

To this day, I avoid the pool with my kids. Of course, we don't have one. We, better yet, *I*, gravitate away from beach vacations. Always have. As the dad, fortunately, I have more than just a passive say in where we spend our vacations. As a parent, like any boss, I have control. I didn't have it over such matters as a kid, but I take full advantage of it as an adult, where I can get it. But the truth is, I only have control over avoiding having to deal with my insecurity, not the insecurity itself.

In this regard, as it is in many cases, being an adult is both a blessing and a curse. We have experiences, insight, and the ability to control our environment. Unfortunately, we too often use our status to avoid, rather than to deal with, our fears. As it relates to our vacation destinations, let's just say that my kids are amazing skiers. We have actually just recently begun making trips to the beach, which my kids absolutely love. Of course, I don't get in, but neither does my hyper-fit wife, which gives me some cover. So far, I haven't had to explain the real reason I don't get in, but I think they know. My oldest, John, is sixteen years old. Joe is fourteen, and Vivian is thirteen. As of today, they, my own kids, have never seen me with my shirt off. My wife—yes, my wife of eighteen years—rarely sees me with my shirt off. If I were to count or list the ways in which this, my most glaring insecurity, has altered my life, my behavior, my experiences, and my relationships, I would never stop writing.

When I was young, my thoughts on the matter were rather elementary. Had I been asked, at the time, to make sense of or explain my actions, I suppose I would have only been internally capable of admitting that I was "embarrassed," but that is where my introspection would have ended—or at least my ability to explain it.

At the time, I never considered the actual reason I felt this way. I certainly never could have imagined the hold that the Chaos Parallel, this seemingly innocuous part of my behavior, would have on countless areas of my life.

In actuality, I still don't believe, to this day, that I have pinpointed the root cause of my insecurity about my body. I'm not sure I ever will, a possibility with which I've come to terms. I have instead accepted the reality that simply identifying and understanding that it exists is a win for me. This is especially true in the context of understanding the link between my actions and the insecurities that cause them. All too often, we start to believe the sometimes ridiculous excuses or explanations we offer others for our actions that are more accurately attributed to something we dare not express to others and are often incapable of understanding ourselves.

The day I could admit that I didn't want to go to the pool because I don't take my shirt off in public was one of the most liberating moments of my life. Gone are the days of perpetually having to say that I have something else to do or somewhere else to be. Gone are the days of forgoing the precious little time and opportunities I have to just be present with my kids. Fortunately, those days have been replaced with contently sitting, fully clothed, in a heavily shaded spot, by the pool watching my kids be kids. I am always ready with an enthusiastic, "Let's see it," in response to their periodic visits and, "Watch what I can do!" proclamations.

For me, the story of my greatest insecurity does not end like a happily-ever-after fairytale—at least not in the traditional sense. I haven't magically outgrown or overcome it, and as previously stated, I suspect I never will. However, growth and life lessons have come from my recognition of it. Simply being able to explain my thoughts, feelings, and actions to myself has been liberating.

Simply being able to explain my thoughts, feelings, and actions to myself has been liberating.

While it may seem like a small win, it is symbolic of a larger quest in my life to make sense of the world around me and the oftentimes intentionally misleading actions of myself and others. The ability to now refrain from focusing on the *what*—and either reacting emotionally or becoming frustrated—I tend to first examine and seek to explain the why.

For whatever reason, framing an action in the context of its underlying motivation or cause has a tremendously calming effect on me. Refusal to examine the why in any situation limits growth. It frustrates progress and improvement. Asking why goes beyond rationalizing our own interpretation of events and forces us to dive deeper into understanding *The Thing Behind the Thing*. It is the direct route to overcoming the life-altering effects of our insecurities.

As a leader—boss, parent, whatever the role—lean into why. While the what is much more comfortable, the why is far more informative. As a boss, ask *why* before every meeting; ask *why* at the end of each day; ask *why* before employee evaluations; and most certainly ask *why* of yourself. Why should drive your business.

As a parent, ask why when your child comes home from school upset; ask why when they tell you they don't want to go to soccer practice; ask why when you make snap decisions, rules, or punishments. And most importantly, demand the answers to such questions to be true, even and especially when difficult.

The ability to understand and make sense of what causes my or others' actions tends to eliminate the noise, chaos, and lies that are necessary by-products of our insecurities. In other words, revealing "why" is the best way to acknowledge and overcome the insecurities that can silently blind us.

For years, I struggled to describe this ever-repeating pattern of unrecognized insecurity that inevitably leads to actions wholly unrelated to the actual source. I later found myself simply referring to it as the Chaos Parallel, which, as defined by me, is a continuum of time, thoughts, feelings, and actions that mirror those of real life, but exist based only on a faulty premise, whether intentionally or unintentionally created. In other words, it is a period of our lives that runs parallel to the life that would have transpired but for our hidden, if not unknown, agenda. It is the result of our failure to recognize or be transparent about what truly motivates us, usually fearing vulnerability. These points in our lives, when we jump the track from our authentic selves to our Chaos Parallel, produce results that are every bit as real and consequential as their idyllic counterparts. However, they are often far more destructive and confusing to others than when we bravely opt to reveal our authentic self.

During the course of our lives, we all spend some time in the Chaos Parallel. Some of us pack an overnight bag, while others of us settle in and stay a while, plodding through a getaway from the realities of everyday life. Others have found a way to transition seamlessly between the two, often mistaking one for the other. But, regardless of your durational predilections, one fact is undeniably true: the tangled web we weave when first we practice to deceive.

The deception need not be malicious, or even intentional. In fact, in deceiving others, we often delude ourselves. Over time, depending on the degree of the deception, we can actually begin to believe the stories we tell—sort of. To say nothing of the inner conflict this creates, the chaos that ensues can affect all aspects of our lives and those in it.

Note that the concept of the Chaos Parallel explored in the next chapter is not the result of a scientific study. In fact, this entire book is intentionally devoid of studies, charts, and graphs that might purport to quantify human emotion. Instead, the thoughts and opinions expressed are observational in nature and are intended to be humanistic and relatable to *your* everyday life. Mine too.

CHAPTER THREE

THE CHAOS PARALLEL

Imagine misplacing *someone* close to you. If you're a parent, perhaps your two-year-old wanders off in a department store as you briefly divert your attention. You start looking around, followed shortly thereafter by calling their name. You soon start moving in no discernable direction, as your neck reflexively extends to give you the impression that you have drastically improved your viewing angle. Peering over racks of clothes, you eagerly attempt to place your eyes on the spot where your child must be hiding. When Johnny is nowhere to be found within the radius you imagine a two-year-old capable of escaping in mere seconds, your heart races faster. As your fruitless search extends beyond the perimeter of comfort, the world grows suddenly larger as the possibilities mount. A week and a half pass in only thirty seconds and you find yourself torn between continuing your independent search and taking the precious time to ask others for help.

J. ALEXANDER GEESBREGHT

As you and your newly assembled team continue your random movements in and out of aisles, your unrequited pleas for a high-pitched response are drowned out by the store's public-address system asking for the same thing. The "this isn't funny anymore" time has come and gone, and the worst of all possibilities is slowly making its way into your thoughts. Your ability to rationalize, remain calm, and even think is starting to fail you. Emotion has consumed you. Instinct has taken over.

Now, whether it takes you three or thirty minutes to find little Johnny playing in a make-shift umbrella tent, your possible reactions are fairly predictable—extreme anger, extreme affection, or, if you're me, both. All are completely understandable. Whether it is your child, dog, or hamster, when you are unexpectedly separated from something or someone you love, it can be disconcerting, at best, and downright traumatizing, at worst. But there are two very important concepts to be learned relative to your reaction to this and other situations. (Three, if you count the one where you learn that two-year-olds are capable of disappearing acts that would make Houdini jealous.)

1. Why are you reacting the way you are? What is the underlying basis of your emotional reaction and the physical manifestations of same?

2. What, if any, long-term effect might your actions have on the other person, those around them, or society at large?

Let's start with, of course, the *why* question. When I asked the question of *why* people react the way they do in that situation, the vast majority of them quickly said one of two things—fear or love. Again, some said both. But, are they right? Or, I should ask, are they *totally* right? Do they fully and accurately grasp the basis of their thoughts, emotions, and actions, and their potentially long-lasting effects?

Few would argue with anyone who claimed they were afraid that they lost track of their small child's whereabouts. However, if that were really the issue, why would many initially react with anger? After all, they just found their child! What is there to be afraid of at that point? The answer is that they were afraid and remain so, long after they find their child. The explanation rests in the fact that while they were, in fact, afraid, they were afraid of their loss of control. The need for control, in all its forms, might well be the most common and harmful of all insecurities. Perhaps this is true because it is both ever-present and the least likely character trait for us to admit we possess; the moniker "Control Freak" is rarely intended or taken as a compliment.

Throughout this book, we will witness examples of how this particular insecurity manifests itself in the lives of nearly all people, at one time or another—often with significantly deleterious effects. Whether we are a parent, boss, or coach, when those in our charge fail to execute according to our plans or wishes, we tend to see that failure—quite subconsciously, in most cases—as our failure. How many times have you heard someone say, "I feel like such a bad parent"? We internalize the dysfunction and see it as a mirror into who we are in that stated role. While it might be a tough pill to swallow, these situations are fundamentally more about ourselves and how we deal with a lack of control.

This brings us to the second concept: the effect. In the simple example of the misplaced someone, almost no one in the moment considers how their actions, facial expressions, and words might be affecting the other. If we did, would it modify our behavior? What if we knew that our child or pet interpreted our response as actual anger or some more lasting feeling of disappointment or dislike? They, of course, don't see our actions for what they are. How could they?

We likely don't see our actions or reactions for what they are. And if we do, we are rarely both introspective and rational enough in these moments to stop and explain the root cause. We are human. We react. But Newton was right—those actions and reactions do, in fact, have their own reactions. However, unlike in physics, when dealing with matters of emotion and human interpretation, those reactions are rarely "equal and opposite." Realistically in the mind of the other, they often take on a life of their own, turning a seemingly innocuous look or phrase into an unintended interpretation and resulting thought, feeling, or action. In short, they can and often do create a series of events that, while loosely based on reality, operate in a parallel universe separate from the true basis of their existence. Hence, the Chaos Parallel.

If we look at the example of the small child, a one-time lapse in judgment brought on by unimaginable fear is not likely to do long-term damage to the child's psyche or development. Now, a pattern of this behavior likely would, but I'll leave that for the professionals to debate. But as parents, we have multiple opportunities over the course of our children's lives to open up to them, model vulnerability, and explain the motivation behind our actions and what causes them. Carey and I try very hard to achieve this with our own children. Our hope is that it will help them make sense of those moments throughout their lives when they find themselves as either the actor or reactor.

After all, children grow to reason and think for themselves over time. As my wife and I are learning first hand being the parents of three teenagers, they even talk back and challenge our motives in the course of the moment. We have learned that, while these moments are fraught with feelings of frustration that often accompany a loss of control, they are wonderful opportunities to encourage our children to respectfully challenge the motives behind our decisions. Obviously, this is a slippery slope that we have slid down many times. While we love watching our kids look beyond the "thing," in an effort to understand the reason for it, there remains the ever-present temptation for them to argue about the decision itself. Like most parents, Carey and I are far from batting 1.000 in this area, but we feel the risk is worth the reward.

Perhaps the greatest benefit that has come from what others might see as our children "talking back" is the opportunity it presents for us to be "wrong," and more importantly, for them to find the flaw in our thinking. At the very least, our practice has placed an emphasis on authenticity, facts, and reason. As parents, we categorically have rejected the "because we said so" cop-out. Admittedly, it would be far easier than what we have created, but our parenting gamble in this area is that we create a hunger in them for dealing with issues based on facts and reality, as opposed to their whims, feelings, and emotions—the elements most often responsible for the creation of the Chaos Parallel.

The bottom line is that we want our children to see the world as it exists, not as they wish it were. We want them to see us as we are, not as we wish we were. And, we want them to see and evaluate themselves as they are, not as they wish they were. Creating and maintaining an environment that encourages, instead of stifles, critical thinking is not easy; and I will be the first to admit that it has its downside. But, on balance, perhaps the only thing I believe Carey

> **The bottom line is that we want our children to see the world as it exists, not as they wish it were.**

and I do extremely well, as parents, is to present, evaluate, deal with, and defend our decisions in the light of day, while avoiding the "I'm the parent" trump card that all too often leads to the devolving of an otherwise reality-based discourse.

Whether you are a parent or boss or both, the truth is that the "because I said so" response is the weakest of all responses, and provides no positive lessons to those we are specifically put on this earth to teach. Shutting down a conversation based on seniority does not hide insecurity, but reveals it. And, while our kids may seem young and unaware, they don't stay that way forever. When they get older, they will undoubtedly revisit and evaluate the methods of fairness with which we dealt with them, and they will eventually find their way to the looming question of *why*? In that moment, they will either remember that we were too afraid to show weakness and vulnerability—clinging ever-so-tightly to the perception of control we seemingly needed to maintain order. Or that we were comfortable not being perfect, but instead used those imperfections to teach the lifelong lessons of authenticity, realness, and being secure in our own skin.

While we have countless opportunities over time with our children to explain the connection between our motives and actions, what about the same example using a family pet? What if Rover runs away? After a similar search, what if our emotions get the better of us and we yell and scold (or worse) the dog for being, well, a dog? It's kind of a rhetorical question since Rover can't reason and I can't, with a clear conscience, pretend to know what, if any, effect my negative reaction might have on him. However, while the list of what I am does not include "dog trainer," those whom I know who are always stress the importance of positive reinforcement. And, while the exact reason for this is probably multi-faceted, I'm left with the likely conclusion, at least in part, that the opportunity for misinterpretation of any negative actions toward them is high, if not probable.

Let's face it, the chances that Rover gets caught, sees and feels your anger directed at him, and then calmly and rationally concludes that the root cause of same is that your reaction is the result of the loss of control you feel over his domain, are less than remote.

To be thorough, let's play out a series of events. Your dog, Rover, runs away. You look for him, see him, and chase him. You eventually catch him. Acting on emotion, you grab his collar, shake it, and yell, "Bad, Rover!" Of course, you tell yourself it's because you love him and that a car could have hit him. Also, you likely skip the part where you rationally explain to him that it is yourself, not him, that you are truly mad at, but that it is too revealing to be mad at yourself and taking it out on him seems like a much more comfortable path. But here is where it gets real. Being a dog, Rover misinterprets your "love" for him as an act of aggression. *Your actions—not your true motives— are all he sees.* He bites you. Draws blood. Emergency room visit, costly bills, the whole nine yards. You have now officially escorted yourself and Rover into the Chaos Parallel.

His biting you was a reaction to a false reality. Your inability (or unwillingness) to see the situation for what it was—and act accordingly—literally created a series of negative events that never would have happened but for a faulty premise. Your insecurity served as the intervening cause of the bite. The chaos that ensued existed in a parallel, but wholly separate, reality; one in which that existence could not have come about without your insecurity.

As the housemate of five rescue dogs (Carey's obsession, not mine), I don't mean to devalue our four-legged friends, but the long-term effect of this misstep is like fifteen years, at best. The better reason to not get mad at our dogs, of course, is that they are dogs deserving of our undying affection at basically all times, as they have for us. But, if we can separate that reality from the lesson it provides, it can be valuable in dealing with the two-legged members of our society.

While being careful to not liken people, or their capacity to reason, to that of dogs, it might be fair to state that, at times—especially when a person has no prior dealings with us—a person's ability to reach behind the thing (our actions) and see our true motivation is far from fail-safe. Just like Rover, people tend to see and react to our actions, not our motives, which is not surprising given the fact that we usually do all we can to hide and mask the root of our behavior.

The examples used thus far have been intended to illustrate how easily we can move from the realities of life to behavior built entirely on the faulty premises of our emotions, but none has really explored the potential depth or breadth of the Chaos Parallel's destruction. Further, each example has been pretty uniformly focused on those conversations, interactions, and relationships we have with an individual and a few others. But what about society as a whole? Could the insecurities of one or two people change the course of history? It is at this point that nearly everyone's mind thinks of the purest form of evil that we know has ever existed—or, at least the one most notably linked to it in our present-day social conscience. We all tend to go straight for the short, socially awkward, deeply troubled, vegetarian painter, better known as Hitler. But I'm going to let you connect the dots for yourself on that one. In the next chapter, rather than constructing a series of events in sequence that lead to the chaos they create, we are going to start with the chaos and deconstruct it to its root cause instead.

CHAPTER FOUR

THE LONG ARM OF THE CHAOS PARALLEL

The year 1992 will forever be remembered as one of the deadliest years in the history of Los Angeles, California, with homicides reaching unfathomable levels. In the five days during the first week of May, over sixty people had been killed, thousands injured, hundreds of houses and businesses destroyed, and entire communities left in ruins due to civil unrest. By noon on April 30, the National Guard had been deployed to many areas of the city and a sunset-to-sunrise curfew was ordered for its citizens. At this point, citywide riots had engulfed its neighborhoods, fueled by racial tension. Just the day before, a truck driver by the name of Reginald Denny was pulled from his rig and beaten within an inch of his life with tire irons and bricks; just one of the many haunting images now emblazoned in the minds of anyone with a television at the time.

Hours before that, the noted flashpoint for what would become known as the Los Angeles Riots had taken place at the intersection of Florence and Normandie. So, what on earth was responsible for this death, destruction, and social turmoil? Well, the answer to that question is multi-faceted and complex and can (and has been) widely debated. But, from a causal standpoint, what was the "reason"? In other words, why did it happen?

The widely attributed and most direct cause, of course, was the event that took place just two hours before Reginald was attacked. This monumental battle didn't take place in the mean streets of LA. No, this war was being hosted inside of a Los Angeles courtroom. On April 29, 1992, a jury found four LAPD officers not guilty of the crimes for which they had been accused. But, if the death and destruction were caused by the riots, and the riots were caused by the verdict, what caused the trial in the first place? More importantly, why did those officers engage in the behavior that led these events to take place?

Unless you have been living in a cave since the early 1990s, by now, you must be familiar with the event that led to the aforementioned reverse timeline. On March 3, 1991, motorist Rodney King was beaten by LAPD officers following a high-speed chase on an LA freeway. Mr. King was extracted from his car and repeatedly tasered, kicked, and struck with batons. The iconic and disturbing images were captured by amateur videographer George Holliday.

If you find my recitation of these events sterile and non-committal, it is no accident. I am not here to debate the merits of the officers' actions or to re-litigate the trial. It is just too complex of an issue, and one for which there is no single or universally accepted answer. I simply want you to see, or at least attempt to see, the whole picture by digging for the root cause of what led to these societal-changing events, or *any* event.

When you watch the Holliday video, whether you see the actions of the officers as justified or excessive, or even if you are in the ultra-logical minority that knows you don't have enough facts upon which to form an opinion, there is one thing you know for sure: the actions of those officers that night, and the decisions that led to them, came from somewhere.

Was the motivation based on strict adherence to law enforcement standards and protocol? Was the motivation the result of fear, on behalf of themselves or others? Or, was it something else entirely? Did the officers lose the control they felt was rightly bestowed on them? Or, was it, as many believe, the result of individual or systemic racism?

Or, perhaps, it was a combination of factors—beginning as a by-the-book procedure that turned into something else, for whatever reason. For the sake of argument, let's eliminate the first one from consideration. Regardless of how you interpret the events of that night, I don't think it is going too far out on a limb to label it less than textbook. As a point of fact, it is worth noting that two of the officers were later convicted by a federal jury of violating the civil rights of Rodney King.

However, slipping any further into the specifics of this case would certainly invoke the law of diminishing returns, as this is a book about looking beyond the events themselves. It's about resisting the overwhelming temptation to allow social, political, or personal norms and beliefs to take hold and shape our opinions of what happened without so much as a cursory glance as to why. So, if we accept—to whatever extent—that the actions, at least some of them, of the officers that night were motivated by something, *anything*, other than pedantic adherence to police procedure, we must conclude that some human emotion was the genesis of what ensued. Be it fear, hate, ignorance, loss of control, or a combination of all four, some human insecurity existed in some of those officers, at some point, leading them—not by force, but by their own volition—to act in the manner they did.

Some human insecurity existed in some of those officers, at some point, leading them—not by force, but by their own volition—to act in the manner they did.

The point is that the Chaos Parallel knows no bounds. Once we exit the highway of reality, the side roads of emotion can lead us in directions we never intended to travel. It is important to recognize that something caused our car to veer in the first place. We either take the wheel assuming command of our destination, or we will follow the path to chaos at the whims of our ever-present back-seat driver, insecurity.

Look, when the worst events in life take place, we instinctively—if not reflexively—ask why. If a plane crashes, we investigate. If there is a food outbreak, we trace it back to its source. When an otherwise healthy person dies during routine surgery, a malpractice claim is almost sure to follow. We have entire federal agencies and scores of courtrooms whose purpose it is to find the why.

Many answers seek to assign blame and punish the wrongdoer, while others provide closure, which allows for emotional healing. But whether the answer has a social, political, legal, or financial impact, each is intended to educate; to correct or end the behavior or practice.

While the motivation to search for these answers ranges from altruistic to greedy, what is curious is just how often we get it wrong, or at least, not right enough. In our stated search for the root cause, we often stop looking at the first sign of a plausible culprit, which is often the most expedient explanation.

If you ask most people what caused the Los Angeles Riots, they would respond by saying some version of "racial tension" or "the Rodney King video." Would they be wrong? Certainly not. But would they be totally correct? Would their answer be complete—the type of complete that leads to learning, corrective behavior, and progress? Would their answer find the *why*?

As the deconstructed Chaos Parallel example was intended to show, it is often necessary to continue asking why. Because, while it may seem attenuated, the answer to the question, "Why did Los Angeles experience its most deadly year in history in 1992?" just might be, "Because four LAPD officers were insecure." Hmmm, I wonder why?

CHAPTER FIVE

TRUST

A t this point, you should have a pretty good sense of who I am or, at least, what I find important enough to include in this book. You are likely aware I care deeply about understanding our individual and collective insecurities so that we can overcome the life-altering effects we're forced to try to sift through. I want you to question everything and everyone, especially yourself; to do all you can to avoid becoming stuck in the Chaos Parallel.

No doubt, you've noticed the value I place on helping others understand who and what they are, as I continue the never-complete task of learning the same about myself. You've recognized the importance of identifying *The Thing Behind the Thing*—of paying attention to the cause, not the effect. And you have seen for yourself the chaos that can ensue when our lives take an altered, but parallel, path based on faulty premises, hidden agendas, and our own insecurities. The examples used to illustrate the indiscriminate bounds of the Chaos

Parallel have ranged from the far-fetched hypothetical about Rover, to the deadly serious account of the Los Angeles Riots.

Consider the chapters to come as applicable. They are personal. Not in an over-sharing kind of way, but in a manner that is intended to feel familiar to you.

If the book, to this point, has felt definitional, consider the chapters to come as applicable. They are personal. Not in an over-sharing kind of way, but in a manner that is intended to feel familiar to you. The examples and people used to illustrate the concepts are as real as you would imagine. They are drawn from a life lived with the intention of minimizing chaos through the understanding of the world and the people in it.

I am well aware of the fact that I don't have the market cornered on success, failure, experiences, anecdotes, and stories. If I knew you, I would surely use your story. But *you* know yourself and you know those people in *your* life that, I suspect, you will find to be nearly interchangeable with those in mine.

The chapters to come are intended to show the interrelationship among the concepts previously discussed, while highlighting one of the most ubiquitous yet underappreciated things behind the thing: trust.

While usually discussed in the context of relationships with those whom we love or work, it is important to note that trust, and its absence, are everywhere. We trust the car will stop every time we touch the brakes; we trust the food we eat has been properly handled and preserved; we trust the pilot of the plane is well trained, competent, and sober. The list is endless. Further, we tend to continue activities and relationships where trust is present, and we tend to end activities and relationships where it is absent.

Trust undergirds everything we do and most of what we think. And trust is never freely given, it is earned; thus it can be taken away and destroyed. If we expect to gain and retain it from others, we must have an excellent understanding of why it is won and lost. But we must first know what comprises trust. What are its elements—its traits and characteristics? In other words, what are the things behind this uber-important thing?

In the chapters to come, you will learn to recognize the universal hallmarks of trust:

- In chapter 6, you will see how what others want—that is to say, their **motivation**—can be as important, if not more so, as what they do.

- Chapter 7 will take a poetic look at the nuances of **communication** and their impact on what others think and feel.

- Chapter 8 is a reminder of why it is necessary to be **secure** enough in your role to have the courage to demonstrate true love—personal and professional.

- Chapter 9 will emphasize the value of being **vulnerable** and the effect it has on others.

- You might find the tone of chapter 10 to be uncharacteristically harsh and disquieting, as the realizations in it were for me. Nevertheless, it will urge you, above all else, to see the world as it is, not as you wish it were. It will demand **reality** when observing life and all things in it.

- Chapters 11 and 12 will pay homage to those who build trust and bring stability to our lives through the ever-present *absence* of chaos they provide. The chapters are intended as a collective love letter to those whose greatest gift to us is the undervalued status quo.

- And chapters 13 through 17 will remind us all how important it is to **recognize and understand the unique traits and qualities** of those in our lives. Truly knowing someone not only aids in our ability to communicate with them by speaking their language, it is a necessary predicate to effectively helping them in times of need.

- Finally, chapter 18 is … well … you'll get it when you get there.

CHAPTER SIX

WANT TO WANT

A s a parent, if you want a quick lesson in trust, harken back to the first time you ever left your child with a babysitter. Remember the anguish, the anxiety, and the unsettling feelings of concern? The only thing that ultimately allowed you to walk out the door, get into your car, and drive away was trust. Certainly not unfettered trust like when you leave your child with your mom, but at least enough that you are able to muster the nerve to leave.

At this point in our lives, Carey and I have hired many babysitters, but unless we are going out of town, we don't even have one now. In fact, we routinely leave the house without even telling our kids, which often resembles a well-orchestrated escape, to avoid the inevitable, "Where are you going?" and the equally inevitable "Can I go with you?" But, of all the babysitters we have ever had, one stands apart from all of them. The Legend of Anna is known, and known well, in our house. "Anna the Super Babysitter" was not only the first, but also the one by which all other babysitters would thereinafter be judged. While we have had some amazing sitters, none achieved the celebrity status assumed by Anna.

Our kids were, well, challenging. Of course, some of that was self-inflicted due to our parenting style. While we knew where and how to push and pull the levers, not all babysitters were equipped to execute our parental game plan. In fact, most of them didn't see or appreciate the pure "genius" associated with what we had created. I'm pretty sure they didn't admire the wisdom in a seven-year-old telling them that the *real* reason she wanted them to go to bed was so she could talk to her boyfriend on the phone. Believe me, there are days when I fail to see the genius, as well. But Anna was different. She was unfazed by their antics—unimpressed with their "wisdom." Always with aplomb, she calmly rose above it.

Anna came from a large family with many brothers and sisters. One of her brothers, Daniel, has Down's syndrome, but the most special thing about his needs are those he has to show love beyond measure and to be loved by everyone around him, especially his brothers and sisters. As she demonstrated in her own family, she was patient, kind, and tolerant of our kids. Carey and I grew not only to trust her implicitly, but also to love her. Even though it has been years since her last "shift," and the fact that she lives five or six rather large states away, we are still good friends.

Over the years, the story of Anna was told many times by me to my employees. The lesson I learned from Anna was not about the evaluation and utilization of a babysitter. It wasn't even just about trusting someone enough to leave them with the most important people on earth. The lesson I learned from Anna was about how I make decisions when the decision itself is of utmost importance. I told my team that while I knew that Anna was in the business of babysitting for money, she made me believe that she would have watched, cared for, and defended my children for free. Carey and I didn't want someone to babysit our children; we wanted someone to *want* to babysit our children.

When it comes to what is most important in our lives, and even those things that are merely important, trust isn't just the thing behind the thing; it is the thing behind *everything*.

BUILDING ON TRUST

When I was building my company, PhysAssist, there was about a ten-year period of time where I was either the only or the lead salesperson. I must note, however, that during the vast majority of that time, I was joined by either Lindsey Edwards or Amanda Buffington, without whom I wouldn't have sold anything. In fact, I never considered myself a "salesman." I almost rejected the notion of it, altogether. My reason for this is that I hated the idea that I, or anyone else, could use verbal skills and the English language to say and promise just about anything, whether or not it was true. The concept of "selling" something to someone as opposed to just telling them about it and them choosing it was offensive to me.

This might sound unbelievable coming from a former trial lawyer, but I make a distinction in my head between being persuasive and selling. I associate the former with presenting what is true and what I believe in and leading people to the correct conclusion, and the latter with convincing people to reach a conclusion that they wouldn't have otherwise reached without my words.

There were many times that I almost dared potential clients not to choose us, but to go with our competitors instead. I did actually do this, but usually only when I could sense that they would be the type of client that I would rather have calling and dealing with our competitors than taking up our time. However, I'd be lying if I failed to admit that, over time, I became perfectly aware that being open and honest about our company's weaknesses was seen by our potential clients as a strength, based almost entirely on believability and trust.

In 2005, we took the small niche concept of "scribes," or physician record assistants, and by 2015, made them a nation-wide necessity for emergency room physicians. Think of them as medical court reporters, or medical stenographers. The need in the market arose due to the federal mandate that forced doctors to use an electronic medical record (EMR), instead of the traditional pen and clipboard to document their interactions with their patients. Emergency physicians were hit especially hard by the new regula-tion, as they were finding themselves spending five minutes treating their patient, and twenty-five minutes "treating" their patient's chart on a clumsy computer with all manner of tabs and pull-down menus. This was incredibly inefficient, not to mention a huge patient and physician dissatisfier.

If the EMR were the poison, scribes were the antidote. We recruited, hired, on-boarded, trained, and managed these scribes who were overwhelmingly smart, driven, hardworking, pre-med twentysomethings. They physically followed the physician into the patient's room, listened to the interaction between the doctor and the patient, and then filled out their medical chart in real time—using their millennial mastery of computers to literally change the face of emergency medicine and the time it took to deliver care in an insanely stressful environment.

One of the really challenging aspects of our business was that it was a brand-new industry. Unlike other staffing companies that provided nurses or doctors to hospitals, scribes did not "exist in nature," as we used to say. Unlike medical school and nursing school, where the individual received their training on their own dime, there was no scribe school from which to select the best and brightest graduates. Therefore, we had to literally make a scribe. It is kind of the difference between a fast-food restaurant that has burgers sitting on the shelf ready to be ordered versus a sit-down restaurant that serves made-to-order ones. From a business model and operational perspective, this is an incredibly significant difference.

Speaking of challenges, earlier I stated that our clients chose us almost entirely on the basis of trust. While this is true in almost every business, it is especially true in a nascent industry that is barely understood, but heavily relied upon by the user to make their business work. Add to that the fact that our work force was comprised almost entirely of the much maligned millennial, and you can imagine the level of skepticism that existed when we walked in a room. But, of all the things behind the thing, trust might be the single most common thread in what makes or breaks any given situation in our lives.

In marriage, or family in general, trust goes to the absolute core. It is the literal foundation upon which a family stands or is destroyed. In business—at least in our business—our clients weren't buying a scribe service; they were buying the belief that we cared as much about their business as they did. Our clients didn't want a scribe vendor; they wanted an Anna. Our clients didn't want us to do a great job for them; they wanted us to *want* to do a great job for them. But demonstrating this to potential clients is nearly impossible in the confines of a sales cycle. After all, trust is not freely given, it's earned. And sometimes you earn the trust of others in ways you least expect.

> **Our clients weren't buying a scribe service; they were buying the belief that we cared as much about their business as they did.**

The first time I remember seeing this trust on full display in business was following multiple "sales" calls with a group in Milwaukee, Wisconsin. From my first interaction with them, I knew they were our kind of people and our kind of client. The two leaders of the group, Drs. Urban and Rudek, were real. They were straightforward with their questions and pulled no punches with regard to their expectations. I quickly grew to like them very much, and wanted them as our clients and partners. This didn't happen as often as you might think for me. You might assume that a growing company would like just about any new client. But we didn't. We wanted the *right* clients. We wanted to like them as much as we liked each other. It was sincerely important to us, and I'm pretty sure that was evident in the way we carried ourselves.

Throughout the getting-to-know-you process, Dr. Urban stressed the importance of a quick installation of the services our competitors or we were to provide, if selected. At that time, their medical group was experiencing the first wave of inefficiency and the financial fallout that came with it, as a result of their newly implemented EMR. They wanted and needed a solution, and soon. In fact, the speed with which scribes could go from not existing in Milwaukee, to being fully trained and working alongside their doctors in the hospital, took center stage in the interview and decision-making process. Unlike some of our competitors, we were extremely accomplished at maintaining the quality of an ongoing scribe program. However, given the early stage of the industry, none of the ever-growing number of scribe companies was very good at the "ramp-up" process. It was an inherently difficult and time-consuming venture. But, of course, like anyone who buys a new service, they go from not knowing it existed one day to wanting it a week ago the next. We were aware of this fact.

Our business, it seemed, was dependent on being aware of this fact, and figuring out a way to accommodate it.

So, imagine the temptation to come up with the shortest of all conceivable timeframes when posed with the question, "How quickly can your company implement a fully functional scribe program?" We knew, because they informed us of such many times, that they were asking all potential companies the very same question. The accuracy or honesty of our response could have easily been influenced by the fact that we knew that once groups had selected a company and begun the implementation process, the likelihood of them changing companies was small. This was due to the complications associated with deleting a program and the protections most companies placed in their service agreements to guard against that very thing. Thus, companies like ours could favorably forecast an optimistically short timeframe in which the job could be completed, which was exactly what the group wanted to hear.

But, was it what they needed to hear? Was it true? And if it weren't, would they eventually find out? And, when they did, even if they couldn't or wouldn't change companies, is that really what long-term, meaningful relationships are built on? We didn't think so.

In one of our last phone calls of the sales process, Dr. Urban informed me that our timeframe was not competitive with the other scribe companies. Our competitors had told his group that it could have exactly what it wanted in six weeks. I remember driving in my car when I got that phone call and looking for a place to pull over and focus on the conversation. After he told me that, my heart sank. I really wanted that contract. My mom and other family lived just ninety miles away in Chicago. I also had family just north of there in Green Bay and had spent my summers driving through Milwaukee on the way to our family's cabin in Crivitz, Wiconsin. Heck, the first

Arena Football game I ever broadcasted was against the Milwaukee Mustangs at the Bradley Center in downtown Milwaukee. How could a California-based scribe company get that contract? I thought it was ours.

Notwithstanding my disappointment, I held firm to our position that it would take nearly three months in order to implement the type of program that we knew would be of the highest quality and ensure the future and long-term success of the program itself. Looking back, that was my form of a test. Clients had to pass our test, too, not just the other way around. They had to value what we valued. If they didn't, they would self-select by going with one of our competitors instead. In almost every single case, this was absolutely fine with us.

> Clients had to pass our test, too, not just the other way around. They had to value what we valued.

As an aside, when I was a kid, I used to go to work with my mom from time to time during the summers that I spent with her in Chicago. It was a metal-stamping family business that my great-grandpa Kaiser started after World War II. Her office, which she shared with about a dozen other people, was a modestly sized room just feet away from a vast industrial plant that housed all manner of massive, loud, greasy dies that could take a worker's hand as easily as they carved up metal. On the door of the equally industrial-looking refrigerator, which appeared to have been manufactured before WWII, was a sign. It simply read, "Do it right the first time." That sign stuck with me. Of all the hours I logged doing menial tasks for German-family-style low wages over the summer, it was that sign (on a refrigerator, fittingly enough) that taught me the most valuable lesson.

I didn't want our company to be "good enough," or to be engineered for those looking for the lowest bid or the fastest implementation times. I wanted to do it right the first time. I wanted to be great. And, I wanted our clients to *want* us to be great.

I suppose I should admit that in addition to taking twice as long to implement our scribe services, we were also quite a bit more expensive than our competitors—double-threat guy, right? Not exactly what the experts teach when suggesting a business plan. Typically, "expensive and slow" isn't a winning combination. While price was always an issue that we had to explain during any sales cycle, as time went on and clients were able to witness examples of our work product in emergency departments around the country, it became increasingly easy to justify. And, while Dr. Urban made it clear from the beginning that price would be a factor for their group, it would not be the primary point upon which the decision would be made; timing would be. Or would it?

Notice how I stated earlier that this phone call was "one of the last" conversations I had with Dr. Urban in the sales process. The reason for the phraseology was because it was not the last. That one came less than a week later and was quite unexpected. Over the years, we were awarded many, many contracts. In my position, I was the one who got to be on the receiving end of those glorious phone calls, meetings, and emails. But none was more rewarding, exciting, and affirming than that one phone call from Dr. Mike Urban. After brief niceties, he began talking about his group's decision, which I assumed had already been made. Then he just said it. "We've selected PhysAssist."

I was stunned, which must have been obvious, since the next thing I remember was him saying, "Well, don't you want to know why?"

Do *I* want to know *why* something happened? Does Rose Kennedy have a black dress? Hell yeah, I wanted to know why.

He said that every other company was less expensive, and more importantly, told him that they could hit or beat the requested timeline, while we refused to budge on ours. But the decision was made to choose our company because his group, very simply, *believed* us. They believed we were telling the truth, not just saying what we knew they wanted to hear in order to appear strong and gain their business. They trusted us.

With those words, any doubt I might have had that we were on the right track went directly out the window. We had our culture— not the kind where people think up a bunch of aspirational words, slap it on a poster, then hang it on every wall in their office as a reminder of all the things they hoped they were but weren't. Our culture came from where it is supposed to come from—a series of repeated actions and behaviors, regardless of who was in the room or what was at stake. We were open, honest, and vulnerable with each other, and we would continue to be so with our potential clients. It was the thing of which relationships were made—lasting, meaningful relationships. By the way, we beat our own timeline on that implementation and PhysAssist has continued to serve and grow with their group to this day.

CHAPTER SEVEN

FOR WANT OF A NAIL

I've always loved quotes—mostly because they remind me of all the things I could never think to say. To keep this book from becoming a regurgitation of all the things smart people say, I will try to use them sparingly. In the most poetic example of *The Thing Behind the Thing*, consider the proverb "For Want of a Nail."

It goes like this:

> *For want of a nail the shoe was lost.*
> *For want of a shoe the horse was lost.*
> *For want of a horse the rider was lost.*
> *For want of a rider the message was lost.*
> *For want of a message the battle was lost.*
> *For want of a battle the kingdom was lost.*
> *And all for the want of a horseshoe nail.*

For several years now, I have had the good fortune and great pleasure of counseling young CEOs and entrepreneurs—usually those with small- to midsized companies. Since numbers have never really been my thing, I tend to focus on human challenges—communication and culture. You know, those little things that get overshadowed by the number at the bottom right corner of a profit and loss statement.

While CEOs have various duties, especially depending on the size and stage of the business, it is widely held that CEOs' primary functions are to

1. set a *vision*;

2. *communicate* that vision in a clear, understandable, and effective manner; and

3. live out that vision through their *actions*.

While I agree with that list, I dispute that they are wholly distinct from one another. In fact, one of them usurps all three: communication. The *vision* itself communicates tone, strategy, and posture. It can communicate the levels of aggressiveness, humility, or flexibility for which the business stands. As for number three, *actions* are the most telling form of communication. Like my thirteen-year-old-daughter, Vivian, jokingly says: "Less talk, more action, Old Man." As a CEO or a parent, we are always communicating something to the ever-watchful eyes of our employees and children. Always.

Actions are the most telling form of communication.

In both our professional and personal lives, those in our charge take their cues from us. They depend on us. They learn from us. They reflect who we *really* are. They become what we *communicate*, not merely what we say. My dad always told me, "It is a poor craftsman who blames his tools." The next time one of your kids reacts harshly to something, take a moment to reflect on how you react in similar circumstances. But children aren't the only mirrors in our lives.

Show me employees who never respond to emails and messages on time, and I'll show you a CEO who doesn't value responsiveness. Show me middle-level managers who treat subordinates as second-class citizens, and I will show you a CEO who doesn't value the equal treatment of everyone, regardless of their title or organizational status.

As leaders, we are on constant display. It is the height of irresponsibility to deny or fail to recognize that truth. As a boss, every slight nod is a reaffirming sign of a job well done, while even the most cursory glance at our watch or smartphone is a universally accepted sign of preoccupation and disinterest. As a parent, what do you suppose we communicate to our children when they are trying to talk to us about *their* game, but we remain transfixed by the football game on TV? If you don't know, call me—sadly, I can tell you. Conversely, notice the joy on their face when you pause the TV, look them in the eye, and ask a follow-up question about exactly how they scored that goal. Oftentimes, the action of listening, or failing to listen, is the most powerful form of communication there is.

It never ceases to amaze me, with all the abilities we have been given to express ourselves, just how inept we are at communicating and how attenuated our intentions are from our words and actions. We, as people, seem wholly committed and confident in meaning what we say, but we are dreadful at saying what we actually mean in a way that is accurately understood by the other. The most prevalent of all communication fallacies is the belief that if we have spoken or written something, we have "communicated." Nothing could be further from the truth.

In fact, every time we talk or write, there is a better-than-zero chance that our words will be *mis*interpreted, which is oftentimes worse than silence. As my favorite line from the movie *Young Guns* goes, "There's many a slip twix the cup and a lip."[2] In other words, from the moment we are motivated to communicate a thought, to our decision to speak, to the spoken word, to the hearing of the other, to their interpretation, there is just so much that can go wrong.

The exact same thing goes for any form of communication. I can write all day, and you can read the words on the page. This only means you have read what I have written. It in no way assures the fact that you interpreted the exact sentiment that I intended.

> The problem with miscommunication, as it relates to our insecurities, is that our insecurities are almost always the root cause of our miscommunication.

The problem with miscommunication, as it relates to our insecurities, is that our insecurities are almost always the root cause of our miscommunication. Again, this book is not intended to cure insecurity, nor is it intended to eliminate its underlying cause. It is merely intended to shed light on what causes some of our behavior and attempt to make sense of it. My sincere hope is that by becoming aware of our tendency to engage in this chaotic practice, we can be truer to ourselves and those with whom we wish to build deep, meaningful relationships, or simply effectively communicate.

YOU CAN HEAR INSECURITIES, JUST BY LISTENING

In business, if EBITDA (basically profit) is the thing, communication is *The Thing Behind the Thing*. If you don't believe me—as the proverb above warns—you might be missing a nail, and your kingdom isn't far behind.

---

2   Christopher Cain and John Fusco, *Young Guns,* directed by Christopher Cain (1988, 20th Century Fox).

I encountered a truly sad, extremely disappointing, and utterly avoidable example of this about a year ago. I was sought out by an owner/CEO about a "problem" with his company, the description of which was as unspecific as it was undiagnosed. I sat and listened to him for about an hour. Within about fifteen minutes, this non-MBA/non-CPA could see he had a cash flow problem. Within thirty minutes, this non-numbers guy could see it was about to get worse. And before the end of the hour, this non-business, business guy could see that the young entrepreneur didn't understand *his* business and that he had no idea what moved the needle.

I started asking questions—focused, but non-accusatory ones. With each question, I allowed myself to insert traces of suggestion and implication. As my questions grew ever closer to resembling directives, each was met with a heightened degree of defensiveness. Remember, *he* called *me*. His posture was not unexpected, though. I'd seen it before many times. Heck, I've been it many times before. I didn't hold it against him as a character flaw, but it was clearly hurting his business. So, what was it? What was he doing, and more importantly, why was he doing it?

At the beginning of our conversation, I thought he had a cash flow problem. By the end of our conversation, I realized I was only partially correct. First and foremost, he had a communication problem. Specifically, he didn't know how to listen. Worse, he didn't want to learn. It never ceases to amaze me when people ask opinion-based questions, then argue with you about your answer—as if they want to think of themselves as open to suggestion, but in reality, are more interested in pushing their version of the facts.

As if his tone and frequent interruptions weren't sufficient clues, he said two things that were the most telling. They gave me an insight into who he was and how he viewed his role. It made me literally hurt for his employees, despite never having met a single one of them. He referred to himself as the "boss" at least five times, and he told me, "Because that is just how it is done in our industry," on at least two occasions. But it wasn't what he said; it was how he said it. There was defiance, bordering on hostility, in his voice. Not toward me, but toward his employees and his own company!

Being the "boss," not leading a company and its people, was the priority for him. Admittedly, I never actually witnessed his interaction with his employees, but you can be certain that they see, hear, touch, and feel what he communicates in every form, every day.

Look, people can have a bad day and they can certainly have moods. This was neither. This was a man who, at the very least, was deeply insecure about his lack of business acumen—for good reason, as it turned out.

Let's stop right here for a minute, though. There is nothing wrong with having deficiencies; we all have them—lots of them, in my case. But it is how we approach them, how we deal with them, and how we account for them that will determine our success and, I dare say, our happiness.

The obvious punch line to this story, the fact that his business continued to spiral downward—although still in existence—is not the point. Merely staying in business is a pretty low bar. The point is that his insecurity about himself and his refusal to recognize its existence and the negative impact it had on his business was destructive to him, his employees, and his company. It was life-altering.

Sadly, even as I tried to help him become aware, to give him even an inkling of opportunity to start working to overcome the effects of the Chaos Parallel, the lines between his present reality and the life he intended to live were irrevocably blurred.

As leaders, we owe each and every one of our employees and our children better. We owe them security. We owe them respect. We owe them self-awareness, as we ask the same from them. We owe them the courage to allow them to pick *us* up when we don't have all the answers, and we owe them the humility that it takes to listen, to learn.

CHAPTER EIGHT

BEING BETTER, NOT FEELING BETTER

The time spent with my company was, without question, the most rewarding professional (and, in some ways, personal) time of my life. Our internal motto was that we wanted to "Do what we know and love, with those whom we know and love." This went for each other, our employees, and our clients. Life was too short to "sell" to people. We wanted them to "get it," and more importantly, get *us*.

In 2005, we had about thirty-five employees in our home state of Texas. By the time I sold the company, we had nearly four thousand employees and operated in thirty-nine states. When we started, my second corporate hire was my brother. The third was my brother-in-law, followed by a series of smart, hardworking, dedicated, and most importantly, trusted friends and acquaintances. While some of us were actually family, we all treated each other as such. We teased, loved, depended on, joked with, and corrected each other. We were honest with each other (I think), or tried to be. And we wanted what was best for each other.

I had a phrase that I repeated at close to, if not every, single weekly staff meeting for over a decade. I drilled into everyone's head, from day one, that it was my hope that we all would "come to work every day with the sole intention of making the person next to them look good."

This was the result of one of two goals I told Carey I wanted to achieve when we started this journey in 2005. The one that didn't happen was the second one. I told her that I would have "everything figured out in two years," and it would require little day-to-day management on my part. Literally nothing could have been further from the truth, as it turned out.

We didn't even make a profit for nearly four years and the following six were the most intense, difficult, fun, depressing, exhilarating, and rewarding years of my life. But, at no time were any of us eating bonbons and watching the dials move from our easy chair, and I certainly never once felt like I had everything figured out. In fact, looking back, I had far less figured out than I realized.

The first goal I shared with Carey in 2005 was—and these were my exact words—that I wanted "the most secure workforce in the history of the world." I had a fundamental belief that if I surrounded myself with honest, hardworking, and trustworthy people who I liked to be around, and created an environment devoid of chaos where they could thrive and learn, there would be no way we could fail. I wanted people to be happy, confident, and comfortable. I wanted them to love what they did and with whom they did it.

However, words like "happy" and "comfortable" should not be confused with "soft" and "forgiving," in the "overlook mistakes" kind of way. We did none of that. We fostered an environment where we were openly critical of each other, but not on a personal level. We were motivated not by making the other look bad, but rather in an effort for them and for us to be better. I likened it to a parent—child relationship. We called it professional love.

Growing up, some of the most dysfunctional families I knew had dynamics where the parents tried to be "buddies" with their kids. As I got older, I saw this behavior as being motivated by the parents' desire to be "liked" or "accepted" by their child, for whatever reason, but usually out of some sense of guilt. This insecurity in the parents led to the evisceration of boundaries and structure that typically exists in the parent—child relationship, for good reason. Due to the lack of restraints and loving, but firm, corrections, what resulted was as predictable as it was surely unintended. The child was actually less secure, as their world and the usual cause-and-effect realities were unpredictable. To me, these kids seemed rudderless and their choices and actions reflected it.

> This insecurity in the parents led to the evisceration of boundaries and structure that typically exists in the parent—child relationship, for good reason.

One night, I was talking to my middle child, Joe, about the importance of not giving up, even though it was far more likely than not that he would never understand the math assignment until he could ask his teacher about it the next day. (It is a well-established and accepted fact in our house that neither Carey nor I is a reliable source for any math-related issue beyond the first-grade level.) After giving him several suggestions about how he might take even a step toward understanding portions of the assignment rather than quit, I informed him that, if he decided to quit, I could not allow him to watch TV or play on his phone or his computer for the rest of the night. A debate quickly started about whether I was "punishing" him for not understanding his homework. He claimed I was, while I maintained that I was merely acting out a reasonable parental course of action based on his decision to quit. I attempted to explain to him that, if I allowed him to quit trying to do his homework because he didn't "understand" it, yet still allow him to enjoy the privileges of a kid who kept trying, I would be effectively lowering the bar on his willingness to persevere.

Somewhere during the course of my explanation, I must have struck a nerve. He said, half crying, "Dad, do you think this is making me feel better?" I paused, got very serious, and said, "You must have me confused with someone else. I'm your parent. My responsibility to you extends far beyond this conversation and whether or not you are 'happy' with me or with what I'm saying to you. My responsibility to you is to make sure you grow up to be a responsible adult who doesn't quit because something is hard. I'm not interested in 'making you feel better,' I'm interested in you *being* better."

The point here is that if Joe had been, well, Joe-Shmoe off the street, would I have taken even a moment of my time to explain this concept to him? In fact, if Joe had been a mere acquaintance, would I have traded the discomfort of conflict to do what I believed was in his best interest? Of course not.

I would have figuratively or literally patted him on the back and wished him some version of good luck. He would have left seeing me as an accepting and understanding "good guy," and I would have stayed off his radar in any negative way. Safe. Easy. Life goes on.

However, this is what separates our actions and responsibilities toward those we love verses those who, let's face it, don't matter, in the long term. With Joe-Shmoe, I'm not willing to risk not being liked or even being labeled in a negative way for what I see as a limited, if any, upside. I have no long-term interest in Joe-Shmoe's success. My son Joe is an entirely different story. My love for him—not my need to be liked by him—is what controls and directs my actions. With those we love and care for—be it a parent, spouse, partner, child, or friend—we should be willing to set aside our personal emotional needs and insecurities in favor of doing what is in their best interest.

Herein lies the greatest epiphany I had during my tenure as a business owner, boss, and mentor. I discovered, over time, that the link between how we express our love for those previously listed and how we express our professional love for those in our charge—if we are doing it right—is nearly identical.

> With those we love and care for—be it a parent, spouse, partner, child, or friend—we should be willing to set aside our personal emotional needs and insecurities in favor of doing what is in their best interest.

Bosses—like parents, friends, etc.—should have the best long-term interest of those who work for them in mind, and that interest should supersede any insecurity that all too often accompanies such a role. The need to be liked is in all of us, to some degree. I have found that CEOs often use the term "respected" as opposed to "liked," which we believe it is a nobler version of "liked." Regardless of the semantics, the reality is that many CEOs, or bosses, in general, are just as human and as needy (oftentimes more so) as those with other titles.

Regardless of what we tell others, or ourselves, every boss wants the coveted *#1 Boss* coffee cup, despite its trite nature. If we are totally honest, our need to be liked, listened to, and followed is part of our need to be the boss. But with this title (or role) comes responsibility, just as the title of parent, spouse, or friend carries with it a responsibility.

Our responsibility to those we both love and professionally love (care for) is to them, not ourselves—not our own happiness and well-being, but *theirs*! If you've ever had someone report to you, think of those who you naturally spend the most time with, those you put the greatest amount of effort into, and those you are the most tough on. They are, of course, the ones you care about the most. They are the ones in whom you believe—those in whom you see the most potential.

So how does this manifest itself in a professional environment? Well, if done correctly, the exact same way it manifests itself in a personal one. We find ourselves teaching in such a way as to reveal the way the world really is, as opposed to a way that makes the other comfortable or happy or *feel better*. Without even weighing the consequence, we move easily and confidently into a role that absolutely has short-term risks to how we are viewed and that can test the security of our position. However, these moments of discomfort are far outweighed by the long-term benefits to those for whom we have the courage to do what is best—for those whom we care enough about to truly love.

CHAPTER NINE

THE STRENGTH OF WEAKNESS

W hen I started a business, I wanted to avoid dysfunction and chaos at all costs. Being liked was not my primary concern; I wanted to be fair, consistent, and caring toward my employees. I guess this is where I write that I wanted to be respected. In truth, I wanted my employees to never wonder where they stood, or how they were doing, or to be unsure about the direction we were headed and the part they played in it.

In order to achieve this, I knew I needed to model this behavior, which required me to be extremely open and intentionally vulnerable. I needed them to see my mistakes, learn how to handle them, and remain hopeful that tomorrow was another day. While mistakes, other than lying, were absolutely tolerated, they were certainly not overlooked. To say they were "used" might be a better description. In other words, they did not come without consequence and correction. But they did come with a lesson; not one of being belittled, but of empowerment from having learned.

There was a humility that accompanied the correction, as well. One that signaled that we have all been there before and lived to tell about it. As an executive team, we tried to send the signal that we weren't better than our employees, we had just made more mistakes than they had.

Unlike with parenting, for whatever reason, finding this humility with regard to business was never really difficult for me. Perhaps because I never thought of myself defined by, or worthy of, any of the titles bestowed upon me in business. I saw myself as a former lawyer who never really liked the law and only really wanted to be a sports broadcaster. The only thing about business that I identified with, or interested me to be perfectly honest, was the people. The people—my employees and my clients—were always my focus.

I let the smart people worry about the bottom line, which, to me, was just a by-product of who we were, what we did, and how we did it. Despite being the sole shareholder and CEO, I didn't see myself as above or more qualified than any of the people who worked for me. In fact, most of them were far more competent at actually *doing* the work than I—a fact of which I routinely reminded them.

But, like most CEOs, I spent most of my life as Not-the-CEO. In fact, most of the jobs I had growing up didn't require me to know the CEO's name. But, unlike many of the CEOs and people I know in positions of power, I never forgot what it was like to be the guy who didn't know who the CEO was. I always got so much more gratification from spending an hour in my office talking with a timecard analyst than poring over balance sheets and profits and losses. A sense of purpose accompanied what I saw as an opportunity to share the good, the bad, and the ugly of my professional life, and how I might help them see their way through a tough situation.

Now, before I go any further down the road of how awesome, altruistic, and morally superior I was as a CEO, let me confess that, over a decade, I led the league in bad ideas. Like, "What on earth made that thought pop in your head?" kind of bad ideas. With the benefit of 20/20 hindsight, I realize that many of my decisions, as they related to strategy and marketing, were fueled by insecurities, competition (not the healthy kind), and even vindictiveness. Fortunately, at least most of the time, the people around me were comfortable enough to tell me that I was an idiot. But not always.

I'm not going to go into how badly I once screwed up our marketing campaign for an annual conference that was basically our Super Bowl, but let's just say that I insisted we go with it because I had a *dream* about it. No need to read that last sentence again, you got it right the first time. Yes. A dream.

I. Had. A. Dream.

What a nightmare.

Fortunately, what I lacked in marketing acumen, I made up for with my willingness to, eventually, admit that I sucked at certain aspects of business. My well-deserved humility and ability to not take my position or myself too seriously were perhaps my saving graces. The reason I mention it is not just to point out one of my few strengths, but to do so with the intention that others will recognize their special place of authority and use it to align themselves with those in their charge, as opposed to alienating themselves. In my free-wheeled, weekly meetings with the corporate staff, which grew from a handful in year one to over two hundred in year ten, I spent far more time talking about how to be people—spouses, moms, dads, and friends—than I did how to be employees. Given my track record of imperfection, as I look back, I'm not sure if I was trying to teach them or remind myself. Hopefully both.

It would be fair to state that my greatest joy from my time with my company was giving freely of myself—my personal successes, many failures, and experiences—to the amazing men and women with whom I spent most of my waking hours. I took as much as I gave, too. I was routinely reminded of just how similar being a boss is to being a parent. The concept that when we are correcting an employee that it should be done out of professional love, with the purpose of making them better, is the exact same principle we should apply when dealing with our kids, but only with personal love. The goal should be the same.

We should use mistakes and missteps as platforms of opportunities from which to teach and learn. Just as with our employees, we aren't better than our kids. In fact, we only know how to learn from mistakes, because we have made them several times ourselves.

We should use mistakes and missteps as platforms of opportunities from which to teach and learn.

However, as parents and bosses—or any position of authority—we often fall into the common trap of first seeking to preserve the power and control (or the perception of both) that we think we need in order to justify the authority we have. Instead of using the mistakes and lessons that we have gathered over time, which are really the only things that qualify us to hold our positions of authority, we project an image of perfection and omnipotence with condescending overtones. I know this, because I've done it.

For what it is worth, it was a trend that Carey and I recognized pretty early on as parents. To this day, it requires us to constantly remind ourselves to remember to admit and use our past mistakes to teach, rather than act as if we never made them in order to be "credible" in the eyes of our kids.

The importance of this lesson, as it relates to parenting, became very clear to me when I reached an age where my own parents' shortcomings and mistakes became known, despite their obvious, if only inadvertent, attempts to shield us from their existence. The profound epiphany I had, in relation to my own role as a parent, was that my kids would eventually know everything anyway.

They will, and so will yours. Believe me, I know well the desire to place myself on a parenting pedestal and preach to my kids about how they should act, be, think, and feel. We seem to convince ourselves that the higher the pedestal, the more power and authority we have over the situation, as if being totally removed from the sin gives us more credibility. *Here is the reality: experience with, not distance from, the sin is what makes us qualified to teach.*

When was the last time a speaker was introduced with, "Here is Bill. He has never done any of the things he is here to talk about today. Put your hands together for Bill"? That's insane. Of course, Bill is always preceded by a long list of firsthand knowledge and experiences. His résumé is what gives him credibility and makes whatever speech he is about to give moderately tolerable.

Have you ever noticed what résumés contain? They are always packed full of accomplishments and successes, wins, and awards. Nobody ever includes that between 1999 and 2003 they ran a company into bankruptcy. Most people don't want to listen to any speech, much less one from a loser, right?

We want the best, the most successful, the winner. They know everything. Isn't this what we do with our kids? Isn't this what we think *they* want to hear—or should hear? Whether it's an inflated GPA, how much we studied, how hard we worked, or how many touchdowns we scored, we want our kids to see us as the best.

It would be too easy to explain the reason for this as simple bragging or taking advantage of the fact that the internet wasn't invented when we were kids, thus totally uncheckable. But, really, why do we do this?

I actually think we are well-intentioned when we do it. I believe we are attempting to set a high bar for our kids to obtain, to create an aspirational norm where mere success is the least that they should accept. When they're born, we think, "I want them to be better than me." So, our objective is noble and just. But then, we spend the next eighteen years trying to make them live up to an unattainable version of us that never actually existed, but that we wish had. Once again, we find ourselves trapped inside the Chaos Parallel.

We tend to avoid admitting that the person we are describing is not us, but rather a picture of who we want them to be. So, again, the motivation is good. But does it produce the outcome we seek?

If we share only the high points, the successes by which we seek to be defined and remembered, what happens to the kid when he or she encounters problems, challenges, and failures?

Yes, the very same problems, challenges, and failures we encountered, but were too insecure to share with them on the front end. If we had gotten out of our own way, could we have prepared them for the inevitable? This is why sincere humility is so important to both possess and model as a parent—or any person.

Besides, I think I would actually enjoy listening to a speech about how Bill ran a company into bankruptcy. In his weak, vulnerable state, I think I would surely find great authenticity and truth. Heck, I might even believe he was the one responsible for the outcome. Why would I like this, you ask? Because nobody ever does it. It would be a catalyst for the authenticity we inherently seek in our leaders.

Think about it. The speaking circuit for CEOs who have run companies into the ground is rather small. Sadly, we routinely miss out on some of life's greatest lessons, because we tend to undervalue those who have failed. But *we* are those people. We are walking, talking, and breathing examples of what not to do. Stories and speeches of great successes are exciting and inspirational. But, tales of woe reveal our imperfections, our humanity, and our resilience. Plus, they allow us to share our real experiences with those closest to us, before they find out for themselves.

As a general rule, we believe that if we appear strong, we will be perceived as strong, and if we appear weak, we will be perceived as weak. Similarly, as people in positions of authority, we tend to believe that perfection, winning, and success are the qualifying prerequisites to having or teaching wisdom, insight, and understanding. Who and what we celebrate perpetuates these logical fallacies in our culture. We are drawn to the front-runner; idolize the strong, seemingly self-assured leader; are mesmerized by those experiencing their fifteen minutes of fame on the front page. So, why then are we surprised when the front-runner is replaced, as it must be?

Why are we shocked when the all-powerful (as if on cue) disappoints us and falls from grace? And when will we learn that the sixteenth minute *always* comes? When will we begin to recognize the intoxicating pattern of success for what it is—fleeting?

It is tempting for us, fueled by our insecurities, to want to be seen by others as smart, or pretty, or savvy, or whatever. But the price to pay for placing undue faith in others, or having them place undue faith in us, is the inevitable disappointment that must follow. With this disappointment comes the erosion of the most valuable commodity on earth, in terms of human capital—*trust*.

Because of this, we have a responsibility as leaders, parents, friends, and colleagues to not position ourselves in these unsustainable roles. Those with whom we wish to build and maintain meaningful relationships cannot trust us to be perfect, but they can trust us to be real. They trust that we'll do what we must to overcome the effects of the Chaos Parallel.

Now, please don't misunderstand, I am absolutely *not* suggesting that we all walk around doing the "I'm just a caveman routine" from Saturday Night Live.[3] After all, successes, triumphs, and wins are all part of our lives and our stories. They have tremendous value in terms of showing what is possible, what can be achieved, and that which is worth daring greatly to pursue. It is only when we are consumed by the notion that our successes, triumphs, and wins are the only parts of our story worth telling that we fail ourselves and those around us.

---

3   *Saturday Night Live,* directed by Dave Wilson, written by Phil Hartman and Jack Handey, featuring Phil Hartman, aired 1991-1996, on NBC.

CHAPTER TEN

REALITY CHECK

There are three ways to get someone to do something. Bribe them, scare them, or create an environment where they are intrinsically motivated to do it for themselves. I was never much a fan of the first two. I always thought that bribing people, or the "carrot" philosophy, would only work so long as you didn't run out of carrots. And I never liked to scare people or use the "stick" method of leadership, because people aren't "following" you if you have a gun to their head. I always preferred the intrinsic form of motivation, which depends mostly on selecting the right people, creating an environment where they can succeed, then getting out of the way and letting them do it. But, regardless of the style, what do you suppose all three have in common? They are all rooted in the basic truth that a person will choose what they perceive to be in their best interest. Always. Now, before you reflexively start listing the examples proving that I am wrong, just keep reading.

Years ago, I made the comment to my dad that everything that everyone does, at all times, is selfish. My dad, who considers himself altruistic, took major issue with my comment. I'm sure it didn't help that he felt I was essentially accusing him of being motivated by profit. Which, to me, was far from an indictment, but rather a pretty obvious point. This does not mean that a business cannot *want* to do good, or that companies don't actually *do* good. It just means that, if all profits were taken out of a business, everything about the business would eventually cease to exist.

By the way, these businesses do exist—they are called charities. But the basic point is that humans are an insanely self-centered lot. Deluding ourselves into thinking otherwise because of an image we wish to project on others and ourselves only serves to perpetuate the Chaos Parallel and frustrate our ability to live our lives in reality. I have grown convinced that the lies we tell ourselves and others about ourselves, and the resulting false narrative they create, are far more harmful to our souls than the insecurity itself.

Do something for me. Not now, because I'd love for you to keep reading, but over the next week or so, think of anything you've ever done or thought of doing that you consider a truly "selfless" act. Anything. Then ask yourself, "What do I get out of this?" If you can answer that question, which you can, it is an inherently selfish act, regardless of the good it does for others. This is not me being cynical, it is me being realistic.

Don't believe me? Let's try it. We'll start with an easy one. Taking your kids to school. For them? Sure, but they are your kids and *you want* what is best for them. You assume school falls in that category.

Okay, how about a tougher one. At the last second, you push your spouse out of the way of a speeding bus, sacrificing yourself instead. It is *your* love for them that makes you do it. Not selflessness.

Still need convincing? Let's try one that's a little tougher. What if you push a complete stranger out of the way instead? This is essentially what law enforcement and first responders do every day of their lives. They get paid, you say? None of them takes a paycheck in exchange for death. But they are willing to risk death in order to do what they love—what they find most rewarding. In exchange, they benefit from being praised for having the honor, valor, and bravery needed to do such a job, which leaves most of us standing in awe.

Our voluntary military depends entirely on the fact that people actually seek out being part of a perceived selfless club: the few, the proud. Recruiting efforts actually play on our innate desire to be selfless, which, of course, is self-serving, by its very nature. So, of course, my dad is in business to make money. There is nothing wrong with that. It's just a horrible marketing strategy and most, if not all, businesses know this. The most beloved (and profitable) companies on earth never mention making money. Heck, they almost act, publicly, as if they are unaware of profits, as if such a motive is beneath them. They show you black-and-white images of the Beatles and Jackie Robinson and encourage you to "Think Different" while selling you a $1,000 phone.

So, what does any of this have to do with insecurities or understanding *The Thing Behind the Thing*? I'll put it this way: my dad, over the course of his professional life, built an amazing company. Through his hard work and dedication, he created the most stable and long-lasting business of its kind in the healthcare world, the likes of which had never before been seen.

I witnessed, first hand, him going way, way beyond his role as owner and CEO to do unimaginably generous acts for hundreds of people outside the scope of work. And he provided thousands of people—people who depended on the stability and longevity of his company—with a place and environment to practice their craft and follow their dreams, for well over four decades.

As for the military and our first responders, I couldn't be more grateful. I'm not sure I even know if I can fully appreciate what it means to be grateful for what they have done for all Americans and me. My father-in-law, for whom I have the greatest respect and whom I love dearly, fought as a Marine in Vietnam at the age of nineteen.

And, finally, I used to hang the aforementioned magazine ad on my wall in law school—the one of Jackie Robinson that encouraged me to *think different.* It inspired me. In fact, I have one of that company's phones in my pocket and probably always will.

All of these things are wonderful in their own right. They are all good. But I believe that it is equally good, if not healthy, to know, recognize, and acknowledge everything for not only what it wants to be seen as, but for what it is. Because, in addition to all the good my dad's company achieved for others, he dedicated his life to it because he wanted to. He not only did very well financially (as intended), he achieved something far more valuable, purpose and mastery. And he was masterful at it.

> **It is equally good, if not healthy, to know, recognize, and acknowledge everything for not only what it wants to be seen as, but for what it is.**

Also, my father-in-law, in addition to his bravery and sacrifice, voluntarily joined the Marines at the ripe age of nineteen, because he wanted to. While almost unfathomable, he did so as the better alternative to staying home following a significantly abusive childhood in rural Missouri.

Lastly, all the good-vibes, clean air, and iconic baseball legend ads in the world don't change the fact that the company behind them is sitting on $300 billion in cash.

While I was building my company, I wanted to surround myself with the smartest businesspeople I knew, who I also trusted implicitly. For most people, finding six people who fit those two qualifications who were also willing and able to serve on the board of a company that hadn't made a dime would have been difficult. But I was beyond fortunate in that and many other areas.

Everyone around me was an entrepreneur. The prospect of doing the same thing was not overly intimidating. I didn't grow up just assuming only *other* people started and ran businesses. My dad, an only child, started his business the day after I was born forty-five years ago in Fort Worth, Texas. My mom, who is seventy-five and the oldest of twelve children, continues to help run her family's business in Chicago, Illinois. Although my parents have been divorced since I was two years old, I was blessed to grow up experiencing two completely different lifestyles and environments, each providing me with their own life lessons.

My father-in-law, after his service in Vietnam, returned to pull himself up by his bootstraps and start a series of companies, including the one he continues to own and run at the age of seventy-two.

When it came time to form my own board of directors, I knew I wanted it to comprise people who I knew would be painfully honest with me, people who had achieved both a level of success and overcome great hardships. Included in the group of seven were my dad, my father-in-law—both extremely smart, successful, and savvy businessmen, despite having completely different approaches—and my wife, who is a former trial attorney and is quite a bit smarter than I am.

Each person—I could write another book about how much I admire them—added a different perspective and level of insight to our growing business. Had it not been such a logistical and emotional nightmare, I would have had my mom on the board, as well. But, for all that my mom and dad did to shield my sister and me from the acrimony of their divorce, putting them in the same room every month would have been a mistake. So, while that board meant more to me than any of them will ever fully realize, and for reasons they will never realize, I also gleaned a great deal from each of them in individual conversations, which I sought out frequently.

Obviously, I talked to Carey about nearly everything every day. From my dad, I had a lifetime of lessons and lectures under my belt, and to this day, I love and cherish every single one of them. While Apple may have encouraged me to "Think Different," it was my dad who taught me to think *differently*—to examine and reexamine everything. He may not have used the same nomenclature, or expressed it in the same way that I attempt to with my children, but without him, my mind would process this world in a profoundly different way. As for my mom, since I spent far less time with her in person over the course of my life, we became quite used to having hours-long phone conversations where we talked about everything under the sun, but usually about either family or business. We share those as our favorite two topics. Recently, it's been increasingly gratifying for me to be able to give at least as much as I receive from her, when discussing business. Really fun.

But it was my father-in-law who was the first to burst my professional ideological balloon. He was the first to introduce me to the cold, hard fact that there is "but one reason, and one reason only, to be in business—to make money." His words. Now, before you are as offended as I was the first time he told me that as we sat at his kitchen counter, let me explain. Actually, no, it doesn't really need an explanation. It's not as if he intended some deeper meaning when he said it. Greg Cooper doesn't mince words and never has a deeper meaning behind them in need of some clarification. He didn't sort-of mean it, or in some bottom-line kind of way behind which there is all manner of nuance. He literally meant that there is no other reason on earth to be in business other than to make money. I was crushed.

You have to understand, I was building a company that had bean bags where meetings were held, that used scooters for transportation around the office, and that encouraged people to dress however they wanted (as long as they weren't interacting personally with a client). We were cool. We were changing healthcare. Doing good. After pleading my case with example after hip example, here is how my father-in-law responded without blinking: "That's total bullshit." Again, his words. I was crushed again.

He continued to make his case, since Greg Cooper doesn't plea. He said, when a person buys a share of stock, they don't care how many rain forests the company is saving, unless they are in the business of saving rain forests. The only thing the shareholder cares about is that her stock is worth more tomorrow than it was yesterday. I thought, "Stop talking. Just stop talking. I hate this."

So, is he right? In a literal sense, probably. Is he totally right? Probably not. But the point is not whether his assertion is completely accurate. The point is that we see both or all sides of what is in front of us.

That one conversation, as disquieting as it was to my naïve business sensibilities, literally changed the way I saw business, in general, and specifically how I saw what we were doing and how we were doing it. It opened my eyes to the way the business world—the real one—operated, and why. He moved me to the limits of a Chaos Parallel I did not even know was affecting me.

Again, pointing out and acknowledging the truths and realities of business motives, the recruiting efforts of our military, or the advertising strategies of worldwide companies does nothing to diminish the upside. It is not intended to cheapen or detract from the immeasurable good that has come from each. Instead, it is to train ourselves to appreciate the complete picture—the one that tells the whole story, lest we be deceived by the proverbial shiny object and intentional misdirection. A reality check is intended to nurture the habit of looking for and finding *The Thing Behind the Thing*. It does not even imply that "thing" is somehow bad or evil; it usually isn't. It is simply an important aspect of understanding and making complete sense of the world around us and the people in it, especially ourselves.

CHAPTER ELEVEN

CAREY

To say I outkicked my coverage with regard to my spouse would be like saying the Titanic had a small leak. I don't mean that in the ah-gee-whiz, false humility kind of way that you sometimes hear; I mean it literally takes people a while to believe we are together.

I met Carey during my last semester of law school. She was working as a criminal defense attorney at the Tulsa County Public Defender's office. She had clerked at high-priced civil firms, graduated at the top of her class, and scored in the ninety-ninth percentile on the multi-state portion of the bar exam. She had all kinds of pressure, especially from her father, to join any one of those firms. But Carey's heart has always been the bleeding kind—drawn seemingly by magnetic force to those in need and less fortunate. It's about at this point when her attraction to me starts making sense to people. Whether it's what led her to work at a boys' home for troubled and abused kids, to serve as a public defender, or her ongoing quest to save all the dogs in North Texas, Carey has eschewed every societal norm, pressure, or effort to place her in the box it would seem she belongs. Why? Because Carey has always known who she is; and, on one particular February 3, I could see it from a mile away.

The circumstance that brought us together was quite fortuitous. I had many jobs and clerkships over my three years in law school, but most of them fell into the aforementioned experience-as-compensation model with which I had become all too familiar. It was late January of my final semester and I was taking a break from screwing around and decided to study for a while. My phone rang and it was a classmate of mine, Mike. He said that he had just interviewed at the public defender's office for an internship and had been offered the position. He told me that they might still be interviewing because of the previous semester's turnover, and he encouraged me to pursue the position. I had no interest in defending alleged criminals at that point, and was about to hang up. However, Mike knew I wanted to be a prosecutor someday, so he said it might be great experience to see how the "other side" worked. That resonated with me, from a strategic standpoint, but I was still not interested. But then he said, "And, they pay $700 a month." Okay, it was worth an interview.

I hung up with Mike and immediately called the PD's office. They asked if I could come in that day, as they needed to fill the last remaining internship as soon as possible. I was at the PD's office just hours later, and after a forty-five-minute interview, the boss man said, "We are 99 percent sure you are the person for the job, but we have to work out a few details."

Since I was downtown anyway, I met my friend Jered at the YMCA to play basketball. When I got home, I had two voice messages. The first was from the PD's office informing me that I got the job. The second message was from Mike informing me that I had taken the job they had offered him earlier that day.

While I knew I had done nothing wrong and that Mike was the one who called *me*, my conscience was still eating at me. I called my dad in Texas to get his take on my moral dilemma. As usual, it was a long and spirited conversation. In short, he advised that I went to law school to become a lawyer and further my career. He said if this job achieved that goal, he would advise me to take it. He was right. But I was still bothered.

My discomfort led me to pick up the phone the next day and call the gentleman who interviewed me. While I was admittedly vague about my relationship to Mike, I needed to know if I had "taken" his position. In hushed tones, he informed me that one of his lawyers had walked by his office as he was finishing up the interview with Mike. Mike had already been offered the job and left the building when that lawyer approached him—the one whose open intern-ship position needed to be filled. It seemed that weeks earlier, at a moot court competition at our school, the lawyer was serving as a volunteer judge when she had an uncomfortable interaction with Mike, who she recognized as the interviewee to become her intern. It was nothing too bad or overly offensive, just not the basis for a pro-ductive attorney/intern relationship. Of course, as you've long since figured out, that lawyer was Carey. The office apparently called Mike back and said they had made a mistake and that they had already filled the position. Obviously, they were unaware that Mike knew damn well that wasn't the case. For those of you who are worried, Mike got over it and I ended up being a groomsman in his wedding.

In any event, I reported for duty on February 3, expecting to be paired with a balding, middle-aged man wearing a short-sleeved shirt-tie combo whose cynicism for the law was matched only by his raging bout with halitosis. So, imagine my surprise when I was introduced to a stunning blond-haired, blue-eyed twentysomething whose smile and pink dress lit up the room.

"Carey, this is Alex, your intern," someone totally irrelevant said. Was this a joke? If it was, the joke was on Carey. Sorry, Mike. My conscience was no longer eating at me. I felt no remorse. None. I *loved* my new job. I was made for this job. And, as fate would have it, *she* was made for me.

After a very brief courtship, we were married. We had a few years of blissful, independent, childless wonder, followed by years of equally blissful children, having three in four years. Okay, the first part of that last sentence is a load of crap. The first years of our marriage were certainly independent and childless, but they were anything but blissful.

We have a saying in our family of five: "There are only chiefs, no Indians." Well, Carey and I are co-chiefs. Rewarding, intense, loving, challenging—for sure. But, nothing about our marriage could accurately or honestly be described as "blissful" those first few years.

Carey eventually made the decision to suspend the practice of law in favor of caring for the kids full time. She put every ounce of focus, determination, and hard work into her new career, just as she had her last. One of my favorite quotes is, "How you do anything is how you do everything." With Carey, at least, this is true. In the nearly twenty years we've been together, her spirit has been unwavering. She is the same person today as she was the first day I met her. It was that first day, in fact, that she inadvertently revealed to me, by far, her most attractive quality.

After our introduction at the public defender's office, she sat me down and went over, point by point, every single expectation she had of me as her intern. She had pages of notes. I swear, I didn't listen to a single word. Poor thing, she had no way of knowing. How could she? It would be years until she fully learned and accepted that I don't listen to or read instructions. After three hours of that (or was it twenty minutes, I forget), we took the first of many "jail runs" together. As we were walking up one of the poorly lit stairwells in the Tulsa County courthouse, I said, "I like your dress." Gleaming with pride, she responded, "Thanks. It was four dollars."

Who was this girl? As it turns out, she is the single most secure human being I have ever met in my life. Ever. And, our marriage and livelihood would come to depend on it.

CHAPTER TWELVE

AMANDA

From the moment we are born and, if we are lucky, until the day we die, we are constantly learning more about the world around us and ourselves. We learn in all kinds of ways—personal experience, the experiences of others shared through observation or stories, reading, television. How we learn, or the most effective manner of delivery, probably depends on the individual.

What has the greatest impact on me might be very different from you or someone else. However, it seems to be a universally accepted belief that negative reinforcement drives home the message. The concept of punishment is built entirely on the notion that one will associate a negative reaction to a particular action in such a way as to deter the original action from taking place in the future. You talk back, you go to time-out. You take the car without asking, you're grounded. You keep showing up late to work, you're fired. You are unfaithful to your spouse, they divorce you. As we get older, the severity—or, at least the impact—of the punishment may change, but the idea remains the same.

As humans, we are almost conditioned to see and compare actions to the potential negative consequences they might produce. Nobody teaches a kid to not touch a hot stove by explaining that if they *don't*, their hand will be fine. They always say that if they *do*, it will be burned and that it will hurt a lot.

For whatever reason, the fear of harm is greater than the comfort of its absence. In other words, we tend to take the status quo for granted. If you think about it, this is true for many of our daily experiences. How often do you drive home from work, pull into your garage, and say to yourself, "Wow, I sure am glad that Toyota Camry at the intersection of 43rd and Bounty Road stopped at that stop sign, or I might not be here right now"? We are well aware of the dangers of running a stop sign. But how often are we cognizant of and thankful for the fact that someone did *not* run one? If you're like me, perhaps not as much as you should.

In other words, we tend to take the status quo for granted.

The point is that the importance of a concept is not always shown through examples with bad or destructive outcomes. Sometimes, showing the positive effect of an action or inaction is just as productive, if not more so. We just need to be willing to pause long enough to recognize it.

It wasn't until I paused long enough in my own life, just a year ago, that I realized that Carey had been *not* "running stop signs" nearly every day of our marriage. That means, almost every single day, I *did not* have an "accident" that could have, and likely would have, derailed our marriage and resulted in the non-creation of a very successful business.

I consider myself a feminist; I have since a few years after college during which I was decidedly not one, nor did I truly know what it meant to be one. I took a women in politics class taught by Dr. Joanne Green at TCU. I was one of only two men (or boys, really) in the class—not that the amazing ratio helped me land even a single date. I might have had a shot, simply based on numbers, had I not made it obnoxiously clear that I only took the class to engage in debate with those I presumed would be vocal, worthy, adversaries. I had taken a gender equality class from Dr. Green before, so I knew what to expect. Despite our political differences at the time, I gained great respect for her, and the lessons and topics we discussed decades ago still occupy my thoughts and influence my actions today.

For the sake of clarification, I consider myself a "second wave" feminist. Of course, I and the rest of America (I would think), support the first wave, which simply fought for, among other things, basic contract and property rights for women. I do not engage in the micro politics of the third wave, but I care deeply about the rights associated with the second.

I have been surrounded by and drawn to strong, independent women my entire life, especially those equally secure in and proud of their femininity. Having a daughter has only served to reinforce my desire to see that she is judged by her tremendous competence, not by draconian beliefs of inferiority by others.

Without really intending to, my actions followed my beliefs when it came to building my company. In fact, it wasn't until about a year after I sold the company (but stayed on as president for about two more years) that I made a mental note of the composition of our leadership team. My brother, Andrew, who was the longtime COO and now president, and I were at the corporate headquarters of the company that bought us. We were sitting in an executive committee meeting in Knoxville, Tennessee, discussing the importance of having more women in leadership positions. I started counting the number of vice presidents we had in our division of the company, and how many of them were women. I leaned over to Andrew and said, "Did you know that nine of our fourteen VPs are women?"

He just looked at me with his Andrew-unimpressed expression and said, "Yeah."

Over the next couple of weeks, as I thought about why our company looked the way it did (in context of the intentional actions to bring about the same result within the parent company), I reached some enlightening conclusions. I didn't hire based on gender. I simply surrounded myself with the most competent and trustworthy people I knew. The reality was, despite the nobility of the optics, I had not formed my company's leadership team with gender equality in mind. I had, of course, done so with selfish motives.

The fact is, I find women to be generally more dependable. Further, it has also been my experience that they seem to care more than their male counterparts that a job has been done correctly. They are seemingly less interested in defending the personal spin they put on the job as a way to justify it not having been done to spec— something I've turned into somewhat of an art form.

I've always had as many female friends as male ones. I prefer Carey's girlfriends to their spouses, almost uniformly. And when I go to my kids' school to eat lunch with them, my two boys are more often than not sitting with a group of girls, rather than with their guy friends. I've recently learned my dad was the same way as a kid. I share all of this with you not only to provide insight and context into what follows, but also to preempt any conclusions you might reach about my motives. I suppose I want you to believe that I come by it honestly.

TWO LAWYERS PITCHING TO PHYSICIANS

The first hire I ever made for PhysAssist was Lindsey Edwards. She had been a longtime scribe and ran the program prior to it becoming a business. She and I were the "sales" team, and Lindsey basically handled everything else. We eventually got her some help (Andrew, Trey, Laura, Raegan, Amanda, and Chelsey), all tremendously important to the growth and success of the company, and each still with it. But none was more important to me, professionally, or more directly responsible for the growth of the company, than Amanda.

Amanda was a former scribe and scribe trainer, which means she was the best of the best. Deciding that medical school wasn't her thing, she took the easy way out, as many of us do, and attended law school. She graduated second in her class and, like Carey, could have had just about any job she wanted. However, prior to graduation, she reached out to Lindsey, with whom she had scribed and installed programs, and expressed interest in joining our corporate team. Lindsey set up a lunch among the three of us, where I had only one question I needed answered. Not surprisingly, it was: Why?

Why would this person forgo a promising and not-yet-begun legal career in favor of working with a start-up scribe company? Amanda was able to convey a cogent argument for why, in a reasoned and convincing way. I tried to talk her out of it by telling her that she would be in my office a year later telling me how she had to leave PhysAssist to fulfill her unexplored dream of being an attorney. She assured me this wouldn't happen. And it never did.

I honestly don't even remember what Amanda was hired to do since everybody just did whatever was needed for so many years. But I do remember what she did the last six years I was there. How could I forget? When Lindsey started having kids, we needed to find a replacement to join me on sales trips. The presentations needed a team of at least two; all the scribe companies had a team, usually much larger and more sophisticated than ours. By then, Amanda's mastery of the scribe position, a more-than-working knowledge of the "medicine" involved, legal training, instinctive business acumen, and her ability to articulate concepts to others in a persuasive manner made her the perfect person to join me on the road. The time that Amanda and I were on the road was the single most dramatic period of organic growth the company had ever seen, and likely ever will.

So, there we were, two lawyers pitching to physicians, the professional equivalent of cats and dogs. Not to mention, we were competing against other scribe companies, all of which were physician owned and operated. Despite starting every meeting with one foot in the grave, we more than managed, though. I was good at what I did, maybe even very good. But Amanda made us great. It took a while for us to gel, but when we did, we were basically unstoppable. In fact, there was a sixteen-month period of time when we won every single contract when we were physically in the room with the potential client.

We weren't gimmicky; we literally never had a PowerPoint or any other formal presentation, and we routinely walked into rooms already full of our competitors' swag. As a matter of fact, while we were talking, potential clients often took notes with the pens and notepads our competitors had given them the hour before. Over time, our presentations became what I can only describe as sponta-neously orchestrated. I'm not a planner, which initially bothered my overly pedantic colleague. But, like with everything else, Amanda learned and adjusted quickly.

We knew which questions we should answer and which to leave to the other. We knew each other's strengths and weaknesses, and Amanda was always good at lowering the temperature in the room when she could tell I was annoyed and just wanted to leave.

Over six years on the road together, we saw every corner of these United States. From Manhattan to Miami, Mobile to Minneapolis, Seattle to San Diego, and everywhere in between. Amanda and I traveled the open roads and friendly skies together. We were gone multiple times a month for two-, three-, four-day trips. On occasion, we would take a week or so and hit multiple locations—renting cars and staying in every imaginable type of hotel along the way. While on the road, there were just hours and hours of driving. Due to whatever insecurity you want to assign, I always drove and Amanda would navigate until I got upset that she wasn't doing something fast enough. We went places we never would have found without GPS. But in all that time, despite an uncountable number of U-turns, we were never once late to a meeting. Never.

We talked about work, life, and ideas. We laughed, fought, and one of us cried, because the other was likely being a prick. If I'm being honest, I had more dinners with Amanda than with Carey over those six years.

A couple years into my travels, I started to save those little plastic hotel room keys. After I filled up my first shoebox, I started filling up another. About a year ago, in an attempt to quantify my travel, I tried to stack the cards on top of each other. They toppled over after reaching about two feet on end. I was standing in my bathroom, surrounded by plastic keys now littered about my countertop and floor. I just stood still and reflected. What I saw at that moment represented hard work, successes, failures, trials, tribulations, unimaginable experiences, the creation of new relationships, and the ending of others.

I took a picture with my phone. Then Carey walked in the bathroom and saw the mess. She stopped, looked at me, and said, "What is that?"

I said, "That is our company. That's what it took to build PhysAssist. That is why we are here."

Carey looked down at those cards, and with an expression that indicated she saw something else entirely, said, "Hmm." Then she walked out of the bathroom.

That was the moment in my life that I paused. See, when Carey looked at those hotel room keys, she didn't see the intense meetings, the fancy dinners, the first-class upgrades, the beautiful mountains of Colorado, and the summertime lake views in upstate New York. She saw hard work and sacrifice all right, but it wasn't mine. Each one of those keys represented a missed soccer game, help with homework, a family dinner, a sleepless night, and just scores of little moments between spouses. They were all stolen by and hidden somewhere in those plastic keys.

Oh, by the way, I almost forgot; did I mention that Amanda is gorgeous? Like, not a little bit—objectively gorgeous. I once told Carey (so stupid, by the way) that I had never in my life seen more people turn their heads when someone walked in a room than when I was around Amanda. I'm sorry, but it is true. It was almost weird. In addition to being smart, knowledgeable, fun, funny, and well spoken, she is just beautiful. It actually prompted me to have a very direct talk with her when we first started doing sales calls together. I should mention that I was never very "bossy" acting. I was always bossy, because that's just who I am, but I rarely took on the persona of a "boss" with my employees. However, on occasion, I could easily transition to that role. Most employees, especially Amanda, could tell by the look on my face that what I had to say was important—or, at least, important to me.

I sat her down in the lobby of a hotel and said, "I need to talk to you about something that I'm sure you are aware of, but I need to say it." Amanda got that, "Oh no, what did I do?" look on her face. I just very directly told her that I had been doing this a while and that there was a better than zero chance that when she first walked into a room of doctors to sell them something, some of them might assume she is there because of the way she looks. I told her that I was sorry to say that, but it was just the way it was. I wanted her to be warned in the event she was initially treated in a way I had seen others treated throughout my career. However, I also told her not to worry about it too much, because as soon as she started talking, everyone in the room would know why she was there—because she knew more about what the client needed than they did, and they would all eventually realize that fact. And they always did.

I intentionally buried the lede on Amanda's physical appearance because I wanted you to see her for her best qualities—who she is, rather than what she looks like. I wanted you to see a smart, driven, hardworking, and competent woman. But now I want you to forget all of that. I just want you to make Amanda anyone that your spouse or significant other might travel the country with, in a similar fashion, for six years. How would you respond? How would they?

What makes Carey amazing is not what she saw in that pile of hotel key cards, but what she *didn't* see—what wasn't represented in the toppled tower of plastic. It's what was *absent* from that pile of memories that makes her who she is. Not once did I come home from a trip and have to answer loaded or passive-aggressive questions, but there was one time that was just too bizarre not to share with you. Other than that, I never got so much as a doubtful look. Now, there were times that my absence was felt more than others, due to the logistical problems associated with a sick child, the electricity going out during a storm, or the time she pulled a gun on the wind at 3:00 a.m., after it blew open the door to our master bedroom's balcony. I always heard about *that* stuff, but usually before I got home, since I routinely called her just about every chance I got. But never doubt, presumption, not even so much as a skeptical or accusatory look.

Okay, I just have to tell you about the one exception to all of that. I have never in my life been so perplexed, frustrated, and amused all at the same time. This was one time when Carey wasn't insecure, she was pissed. Very pissed. And, by all logical accounts, she had good reason to be. My constant defense—which was nonexistent—along with my genuine laughter at my inability to explain the circumstance did not help. So, here's what happened:

I got home from a trip and started unpacking in our closet. Of course, Carey usually hung out with me in there as I filled in the gaps about my meetings and travels. While I was separating dry cleaning from dirty laundry, I pulled out one of the white dress shirts I had worn to one of my meetings. The collar had red smudge marks all over it. I mean *all* over it. Carey said, "What the hell is *that*?" I had never before heard that tone in her voice, and thankfully, I haven't heard it since.

I stared motionless with my mouth agape, holding my shirt in one hand while the other was palm up making the universal sign for "I have no clue." That wasn't working. She grabbed the shirt as I started to feverishly search my bag for an exploded pen, drink, anything!

Knowing that I was innocent of the charges being levied by Carey's entire physical countenance, I did what anyone in my position would have done: I started laughing. There was not a single logical defense or explanation for this amount of what appeared to be makeup or lipstick on my dress shirt collar. Not one—and I can usually come up with *something* in nearly any situation. I had nothing, and it showed.

My mind went to some very strange places. Had I been drugged? What? No! That was insane, but so was the shirt, so I kept going. Had Amanda played a sick—albeit damn funny—joke? Not likely, but I kept that one open as a possibility since nothing else was coming to mind. Meanwhile, Carey's angered face was turning a nice shade of "get the hell away from me," which complemented the unaccounted-for smudge marks on my shirt. She exited the closet, then the bathroom, and then our bedroom. I listened for a slamming door to the garage downstairs, but thankfully I never heard one. I just sat there, my mind racing, while still acknowledging, from Carey's point of view, how this looked. I was nonplussed.

I stayed upstairs trying to come up with something to say without laughing, but to no avail. I finally went downstairs, but when I got within ten feet of her, I could actually feel the force field repel me away. I went into the living room and sat down for a while before going back upstairs determined to figure this out. I wasn't ever worried, I had no reason to be. Still, how would Carey ever *know* know that?

I stared at my clothes, my bag, and the things around it that I had already unpacked. Then I saw it—the culprit. I lunged for my shoes like they were a flowing oasis in the desert. I had packed my shoes in red felt-like covers. Either condensation or just some liquid had gotten them wet and the dye had made its way to my shirt. Seriously. But now I had to *prove* my theory before approaching Carey because I knew I was only going to have one shot. Without regard for the newness or whiteness of our towels, I grabbed one off the shelf, ran the shoe cover under the sink, and rubbed it on the towel. Vindication!

There are eighteen steps from our upstairs to the downstairs; I *might* have taken three of them. Screaming the whole way, I ran up to Carey, who was in the kitchen, and I said, "I figured it out!" I turned on the kitchen faucet and conducted the same test I had done upstairs. I froze waiting for that look of forgiveness or relief or whatever on her face, so I could start breathing again. She took a breath, as if to speak. The verdict was in. I was about to win my first and only criminal defense trial. It was my Perry Mason moment!

Carey looked at me, then at the evidence, and said, "You ruined a towel for this?" With that one sentence, she managed to simultaneously forgive me and make me feel as if she never doubted me for a second. Amazing. She is truly amazing.

So, with the notable exception of that one instance, I never had to pay for being gone. As the years since my travel have gone by, I find myself increasingly grateful to Carey for what she didn't do—for what she could have done. I also find myself increasingly cognizant of the effect it could and would have had on me, on us, and on our business.

Going back to when we were first married, I would hear friends talk about how they had to be home by this time, or how their wives wouldn't let them do whatever. I remember years ago trying to get one of my good friends to go somewhere with me. When I questioned why he couldn't go, I remember him saying, "Not everyone is married to Carey." He had that right.

What strikes me most are the times I think of how different life could have been. How would I have been had the shoe been on the other foot, so to speak?

Let me put it this way: while I was writing this book, I arranged for Carey and her friend Noel to take a girls' trip to LA for Carey's birthday. I had been spending some time out there writing and thought it would be a good opportunity to give her a break from the everyday. By all accounts, they had a great time. I got text updates, calls, and pictures. She tried to manage my management of the kids' schedule from fifteen hundred miles away, but I just wanted her to have fun. I told her I had this.

The second night they were there, she sent me a picture of them eating at a fun restaurant. I looked closely at the picture; something was missing. I texted her back a snarky, "Did you forget your ring?"

She wrote back, "Ha," as if I had just written something funny. I was sure I had not. But I did think, "How ridiculous is this?" Am I actually insecure about Carey not having her ring on? Noel had her ring on. Why didn't Carey? But instead of just asking her, I was less than engaging the next few times we spoke.

Finally, she asked, "Are you okay? You seem a little off?" I somewhat embarrassingly explained. She laughed and said, "Honey, have you not noticed that I have been unable to wear my ring for six weeks? The band was literally digging into and cutting my finger."

I admitted that I had, in fact, *not* noticed that little gem of information, but that I was sorry. Just like that. A picture. That's all it took for me to expose my underlying insecurity that I didn't even think was there. I have done just about whatever I have wanted for two decades, then Carey goes out of town for three minutes and I make her pay for something she didn't even do. So, what if the shoe had been on the other foot? Well, in reference to our business, there just wouldn't have been one at all.

Could you imagine working your butt off, managing a company, flying around from city to city, meeting to meeting, having to be "on" all the time, and then coming home to someone who questioned who you are and what you had been doing? Or worse, what if that were the reception you got when you called from the road to check in and tell everyone that you loved and missed them? Can you imagine how impossible it would be to function at the top of your professional game in that personal environment? Eventually the music would stop, right?

If Carey had done this, I can state with certainty that I would have resented her immediately. No one likes to be questioned or accused of something they didn't do, and I am at the very top of that list. Had she done so, or even come close to doing so, it would have led to nonstop fighting and inevitable resentment, not to mention the example we would have been setting for our kids. There would have been no PhysAssist, at least nothing resembling what we built. But, far more importantly, there would have been no us. I'm certain of it.

So, even the absence of one's involvement in the Chaos Parallel can be life altering. But to get there, you have to first know that it exists. Most of us aren't natural-born Careys, but we can get there, if we learn to pay attention to those simple insecure nuances that motivate our actions, inactions, and day-to-day thoughts.

Every day that I went to work, whether in town or across the country, it's what Carey *didn't* do that allowed me to succeed. The security she had in herself and in me allowed me to focus on building a business during those incredibly important times. Every single day, Carey didn't run a stop sign, there was no accident, I didn't touch the stove, and my hand was fine. She, through her sense of self and (I hope) a sense of who she married, built and nurtured a constant state of the status quo.

Today, I am making a sincere effort to recognize and be thankful for the utter absence of chaos she provides, as well as seeking to eliminate the noise I might be inadvertently creating. As destructive as insecurity can be, the benefits of security in oneself can have a meaningful, life-sustaining effect.

CHAPTER THIRTEEN

IF YOU KNOW A ...

F ew things in this world feel as helpless as watching someone you love experience pain. Of course, there are different kinds of pain and different kinds of remedies. Physical pain can often be fixed or healed, usually with the help of a healthcare professional and the irreplaceable benefit of time. But unlike most physical ailments, some emotional wounds never heal. Some are temporary, but some have a lasting impact on who we are and how we see the world, others, and ourselves.

I, like most of you, am not a mental health professional. But when it comes to the day-to-day interactions with those I love, I am even *more* qualified—and so are you. I am a friend, a child, a spouse, and a parent. In other words, I have a vested interest in the daily lives and well-being of those closest to me, thus inherently and imminently qualified to assist. What's more is that my special position as someone who they love and trust affords me not only the opportunity, but the privilege of doing whatever I can to usher them through whatever difficulty they might be experiencing. In this sense, I am not helpless at all. This in not to suggest I have all the answers—of course, I do not. But I am, we all are, far from helpless.

Since those in our lives come in all shapes, sizes, and temperaments, each requires a slightly different form of communication. While none of us has all the answers, nor is it even possible for us to fix all problems, there is something we are all capable of doing. Armed with years of experience, comprising success, failure, and lessons learned, we can help those we love to understand the past and, more importantly, we can provide context for the future. In other words, we, by our very existence—having lived through all manner of hardships and setbacks—are living examples of the greatest gifts we can give another: *hope*.

> We, by our very existence—having lived through all manner of hardships and setbacks—are living examples of the greatest gifts we can give another: hope.

If there *is* a downside to youth, it is that tomorrow often seems unattainable, as young lives are often stuck in a perpetual state of today. But the uncertainty of tomorrow can be allayed by making sense of yesterday. In fact, our lives are proof that we made it through yesterday and are thus capable of finding our way to tomorrow. And as helpless as we may be to change the what, we are imminently capable of explaining the why—a wonderfully effective source of peace.

When I was a kid, I went to my dad with almost every problem I had. And if I didn't go to him, he usually sought me out; I was inept as a kid as I am now about suffering in silence. He loved to convey the wisdom he accumulated from his dad and his many life experiences. He loved to lecture me—still does, actually. But unlike most kids, I loved to listen—still do, actually. Truly love it. When I was hurting, like most parents, he would try to console me, but not for very long. That was never really his thing. He was much more pragmatic, which worked well for me, given my personality. He did, on occasion, fall into the trap of jumping directly to a conclusion, as many adults (especially male) tend to do. But for the most part, he broke down my issues to their simplest form. For a very complex thinker, he continues to have a remarkable ability to simplify everything in a way that reveals its essence. He is masterful at this. And while I never once remember him specifically encouraging me to understand *why* something was happening, or *why* someone was treating me the way they were, looking back, that is exactly what he was doing.

As a general rule, he was never really that concerned with the problem du jour. Instead, he focused on me—my assessment, interpretation, and understanding of what was going on, not what was going on, itself. In other words, it was my dad who taught me to examine *The Thing Behind the Thing*—something I didn't realize until very recently.

As the parent of three kids who are all in their prime everything-is-a-minor-crisis years, I now recognize certain tendencies I have in my weakest counseling moments that remind me of my dad during his. Looking back, I now recognize that intense, if not somewhat irrational, focus he got that now comes over me at times where all I want to do is deal directly with the little brat at school who is causing my child pain. Fortunately, these emotive ramblings are usually as short lived as they are counterproductive.

Like I did, my kids have learned to just let me get it out as they wait for the constructive guidance. When it does come, it is usually in the form of explaining to my kids the *why*. As I tell them all the time, I can't fix their problem, but I can influence their understanding of it. Again, simply having a place to put the behavior of another, in terms of its source or motivation, can bring a sense of peace to a child. At least it did for me and seems to for my kids, as well.

Carey and I learned early on that our kids, and the manner in which they respond to and deal with adversity, are as varied as if they were from three different families. In talking to others, I've recently learned that this is not at all uncommon for couples with multiple children, so I'm much nicer to the mailman now. I've long said that raising my oldest son, John, is like raising a combination of my dad and my father-in-law. Raising Joe is like raising myself. And raising Vivian is like raising a perfect combination of Carey, Carey's mom, and me. Each has their challenges, and of course, their great rewards.

I will issue the following preface, if not disclaimer, before continuing. I realize that not everyone in the world has kids. However, my sincere hope is that this next part will be eventually applicable, in some way, to everyone. It's important to remember, as I'm sure you've noticed by now, that every person used to illustrate a point in this book need not have an exact counterpart in one's own life. So, again, not everyone will glean the same message from the same thing. In fact, it would be odd and surprising if they did.

As is the case with most people, my wife, kids, family, friends, and coworkers—many of whom are represented in this book for an intended purpose—are my orientation to this world. They are my mirrors—each reflects back, in their way, who I am and how I live my life. As has been the case to this point in the book, the next few brief chapters are intended to be illustrative of our need to see and understand people not for *what* they are or even *who* they are, but *why* they are.

Being able to identify *The Thing Behind the Thing* when it comes to politics, or a company's marketing strategy, or life's events and challenges is helpful—very helpful in many cases. However, seeing the very essence of a person is the cornerstone of our ability to communicate effectively with them and build deep, meaningful, and lasting relationships.

CHAPTER FOURTEEN

IF YOU KNOW A JOHN

John is an old soul. Always has been. He is imminently logical and rarely, if ever, shares his emotions, especially painful ones. He, like his grandpas, finds it very difficult to be vulnerable—to show what he sees as weakness, in himself and others. But being unable or unwilling to share or express one's pain does not obviate its existence.

John, while mature beyond his years, is not immune to the pressure and pain of simply being a teenager. This has made my ability to help in moments that I *know* are painful for him very difficult. As it relates to John, I often do feel powerless—yes, helpless—wanting only to speak his language, with less than stellar results. If I'm being honest, I do not feel like I am serving my eldest son the way I should. In fact, I feel that I am failing him in some sense. But it is not from a lack of trying, to be sure.

Every time we do talk, I marvel at his insight, which, unlike some of us, he doesn't feel the need to express every moment of the day. He is content in his own skin and seems to prefer his own thoughts to those of others, which, if I were John, I would as well. He sleeps outside whenever or wherever we let him. All he wants to do is go camping, but until last week, has never once asked me to take him. It's because John can read a room and a person better than any adult I know, and he is well aware of the fact that my idea of camping is when room service at the Four Seasons forgets to put clean sheets on the bed. I learned this about John when he was only six years old.

I was driving back to the house one Saturday with a large to-do list on my mind. John was in the back seat. We had just turned the corner revealing the large signage for Academy Sports and Outdoors in the distance.

A moment later, John said, "Dad?"

Rather curtly, I said, "What?"

After a few seconds of silence, a sweet little voice from the backseat said, "Never mind."

About five minutes later I just smiled, finally replaying in my mind the brief but informative "conversation" we just had. I said, "John, you were going to ask me if we could go to Academy, weren't you?"

"Yes," he replied.

"Why didn't you?" I inquired.

"No reason," he said. Incredible. But the fascinating thing was not that he knew that my answer would be no based only on the tone of my voice from the previous question; it was that he didn't want to reveal his method for knowing it.

As we both get older, I just continue to talk to John and listen whenever given the chance. I am slowly building trust with him—I think—through the demonstration of my own vulnerability and imperfections. John is a kid of many thoughts and few words. Oftentimes, what he doesn't say is as telling as what he does. I am learning to speak his language, which, unlike my native tongue, usually involves little talking.

His words, when he does use them, must be guarded as sacrosanct—a lesson I learned through observation and fortunately, someone else's mistake. Unfortunately, that someone else was Carey. John once confided in her who he "liked" at school. Not thinking it was a state secret, she told her mom. When word got back to John, it was as if Carey had ripped open his chest and pulled out his heart.

Note to self: revealing a kid's secret—even a seemingly innocuous one—can have a lasting negative impact on one's ability to connect. In some ways, John is no different from the rest of us. He too needs to have faith and trust in those with whom he wishes to build meaningful relationships. He, and people like him, just have a higher bar than most of us for what qualifies as a breach of that trust.

If you know a John, revel in their differences. Be amazed by them. Don't seek to change them, but instead let them change you.

If you know a John, revel in their differences. Be amazed by them. Don't seek to change them, but instead let them change you. I continue to learn from John, as I have since the day he was born. I truly admire him for everything he is: all the things I wish I were. John is my hero. I hope to be more like him when I grow up. By the way, we are going camping next Saturday afternoon. I expect to spend all morning at Academy.

CHAPTER FIFTEEN

IF YOU KNOW A JOE

J oe, on the other hand, is both the easiest and most difficult child for me to raise. This is largely due to the fact that he *is* me, which serves for me as both a constant ego trip and a perpetual state of anxiety. I can literally tell what he is thinking by a look in his eye or an expression on his face. I once shared that with him.

I swear on everything that is holy that this is true: He said, "Okay, what am I thinking?" Without flinching, I proceeded to tell him, in great detail, not only what he was thinking, but why he was thinking it. He stood motionless, amazed by my superpower and fearful of its ramifications. Joe, unlike John, not only expresses every emotion he has while making no attempt at all to hide them, he does so with all the passion and intensity of a lawyer making his last plea to the Supreme Court. He feels everything deeply and sincerely. He is an insanely kind and caring child with the ability to light up every room he graces, along with all the lucky souls in it. His ability to genuinely appreciate everything, and express as much, is a constant reminder to anyone around him that being genuinely happy is its own reward.

His personality allows him to have and experience great triumphs; Joe was seemingly who Teddy Roosevelt was picturing when he wrote about the Man in the Arena—always willing and eager to dive, headfirst, into any situation. In fact, we have a phrase in our family to describe Joe. It is: "Ready. Fire. Aim." My dear God, I love that kid.

However, these beautiful traits come at a cost. There is a price for admission to the never-ending play that is Joe. His openness and unabashed sincerity on the front end leave him ever exposed and vulnerable to heartache, discouragement, and disappointment on the back end. In his moments of sorrow, I both deeply identify with and hurt for him. I not only empathize with him in his times of trouble, I can predict them—I actually see them coming.

Where I am constantly reacting to John—doing my best to be what he needs when he needs it—with Joe, I often feel like a guy watching a movie I've seen a hundred times before. This causes a great dilemma for me: Do I let him experience the disappointment that comes to those who fundamentally believe everyone is as well motivated as him? Or, do I constantly warn him about everything this world is capable of doing to someone who is such an open book? If so, how much? When?

If so, how much, and when are all questions to be answered on an individual basis. But I will offer this encouragement: If you know a Joe, just be proud of him or her. Believe in them. Stand in awe of the fact that they refuse to bow to a cynical society that teaches that they must conform or else, that the only way to be happy is to hide it, lest anyone take advantage of what could be perceived as weakness. If you know a Joe, take stock. Your Joe, just like mine, will be fine.

We should all be so lucky to be a Joe. I count myself blessed beyond measure that I have my own.

CHAPTER SIXTEEN

IF YOU KNOW A VIVIAN

A nd then there is Vivian, my favorite, to hear her tell it. Not only is she nothing like her older brothers, she is like no other person I know. She is literally the most interesting person I've ever met. At the age of thirteen, she is already the most determined and focused individual in my life. And she is tough in every way.

The first time I ever heard one of my kids tell me no and mean it was from Vivian. I told her to go to bed one night when she was three years old. It had been a nightly routine for nearly seven years at the time. But unlike John, who used to ask us if he could "go to bed yet," or Joe, who we could easily shame into going to bed, Vivian was never so compliant. Ever. I said, "Go to bed, Vivian." And as long as I live, I will never forget this moment.

She turned around, wearing only a diaper, looked me directly in the eye, and said, "No!"

What? No? What did that mean? Kids don't say no when you tell them to go to bed. They stall. They plea. They take their sweet time walking up the stairs as they think of just one more question they have to ask you. But they don't say, "No!"

Silly us, we had no idea that the rules didn't apply to Vivian. Even when they did, she had a way of making it seem as if they were on her terms. Except for a very brief departure, "time-out" was our punishment of choice for our kids. The kids had to sit on the stairs for some random amount of time if they disobeyed us. Much to our surprise, Vivian would actually go to time-out. But it was the way she did it that revealed who she was. She usually didn't have to be told.

Here's how it would go:

Carey or I would tell her to not do something. If Vivian wanted to do that thing, which she typically did, she would just do it. Then, looking right at us as if to dare us to change the rule, she would casually walk over to the stairs and put herself in time-out. It was both hilarious and infuriating.

Until she started to value her time more, time-out was pretty pointless for Vivian. Carey read all kinds of books on "stubborn" or "strong-willed" children. Some of what she read and some in our social circle, at the time, as well as our own upbringings, led us to consider spanking as a form of punishment. We tried it—"tried" being the operative word. The experiment lasted about twenty seconds, if that, and Vivian was the reason why.

First of all, John never really needed punishment. When he was old enough to know better, he didn't really do very many things wrong. And when he did, we literally just had to tell him not to do that thing and it was pretty much over. Carey tells me that is an optimistic view of reality, but it sure felt that way. Joe, on the other hand, was always getting into something. But he was so sensitive, all we had to do was look at him and he felt badly enough to stop, if only temporarily.

But Vivian, of course, was a different story. I tried to spank Vivian once. *Once.* We told her to do something. She refused and carried on. So, I spanked her through her diaper. Again, just the diaper, there was no actual clothing on this kid for like 90 percent of her childhood. Honestly, I am not making this stuff up. I spanked her and she turned her head around, and with an angry look on her face, she said, "That. Didn't. Hurt."

Three years old.

Carey, who had been watching the inaugural spanking, ran out of the room laughing so hard that she had tears rolling down her face by the time I joined her. When I finally recovered from the abject parenting disaster I had just witnessed—or created—I looked at Carey and said, "The balls on that kid!" Given that I was unwilling to spank my daughter hard enough to actually hurt her, spanking was off the table. Viv won again. We, as well as the world, were going to need to get used to that.

Taking only after her mom, Vivian is a great student. Taking after her dad, I'm not sure she actually cares about school, but she just refuses to let anyone beat her. After failing four straight years to be elected to student council, she ran again this year. Carey and I just shook our heads and said, "She won't quit."

On the day of the election, as we were preparing our annual "we are proud of you for trying" speech, we received a text from someone at the school informing us that Viv had actually been elected. We were ecstatic. But the celebration we were planning to have when she got home was quickly cut short by a barely content Vivian. Seconds after giving her the hug I had built up for five years, she said to me, "Now I want to be student body president." Ugh. Why couldn't this kid leave well enough alone? Just take the "W" and move on, like everyone else. Not Viv. And a week later, after rapping her speech in front of the entire school, she won.

In addition to eventually succeeding at just about everything she sets her mind to, Vivian is an extremely talented, hardworking, and accomplished soccer player. And despite her pint-sized frame, she is as physically tough as she is mentally determined. That girl has been kicked in the face with the ball more times than I've played soccer, usually drawing blood or breaking her nose. A couple years ago, she refused to come out of a game after being kicked so hard in the face you could hear the gasps from the crowd on the next field over. With blood pouring down her mouth and chin, she waved her coach off the field and said she was fine and wanted to keep playing. However, the referees, who are now charged with players' safety, felt differently. Nearly everyone was horrified by the visual. But this was at least the fifth time that Carey and I had witnessed blood coming from our daughter's face since she started playing at age three. Had it been one of our boys, they would have been carried off on a stretcher. But it was Vivian, so we knew she would be fine.

Finally, despite the normal stereotype of preteen girls, Vivian has never done drama. She is well aware that it exists and even seems to be mindful of the fact that she is expected to engage in it. But she doesn't. She has told me many times about the petty (and totally normal) squabbles among her classmates. I wouldn't characterize her emotion toward it as disdainful or even judgmental. But she has always seemed to just rise above it, as if it was not worthy of her time or energy.

So, I have this tough, smart, determined, talented, willful child. She is neither repressed, nor overly demonstrative. A child who, like her mother, knows exactly who she is, regardless of what the world around her expects she should be. She is as close to unflappable as a thirteen-year-old gets. But she is *not* unflappable. She *is* thirteen. And, every time I think I have Vivian sussed, she reveals another side. It's fascinating.

We all have our insecure moments and they are as real to us as they are different from others. As you will see, Vivian, for the first time ever, was no exception. As I

We all have our insecure moments and they are as real to us as they are different from others.

was recently reminded, little girls—even tough ones—need their daddies, often at times and in ways we least expect.

CHAPTER SEVENTEEN

WE PURSUE THAT
WHICH RETREATS

About a year ago, Carey was out of town with Joe and I was the sole chauffeur, which I was highly qualified for. I was the sole cook, which I delegated to local eateries, and sole counselor, which, as it relates to Vivian, is almost never needed. On the rare occasion that something is bothering her, she usually seeks out the advice of Carey, reserving me for pregame pep talks and bad rap duets with the top down.

Carey left me all sorts of detailed notes and reminders about where I needed to be, at what time, and whom I was either taking or picking up. On this day, I was charged with taking Vivian and her teammate Mak to soccer practice after school.

"Don't be late," the note read. About thirty minutes before we needed to be there, Viv was upstairs getting ready—or so I thought. As I was talking to John downstairs, we heard Vivian crying—

bawling, actually. John and I immediately panicked, as we both were well aware of what it took to make Vivian cry.

John bolted upstairs as I screamed, "Vivian, are you okay?"

Before she could answer—not that she would have—John yelled back, "She's fine." But what he meant was that she was not physically injured.

When I got to her room, John was sitting on her bed with his hand on her back trying to console her in his I-don't-see-anything-wrong-with-you kind of way. I said, "Bibby, what's wrong?" She was staring at her iPad, but wouldn't or couldn't respond. I looked at the iPad for answers, but it seemed she had been texting Carey. By the looks of it, Carey had been begging for Viv to tell her what was wrong, as well, but to no avail. All I could gather was that some girls had been mean to her that day at school. Not just a little mean. Several of them told her that they hated her for something she did not do. Clutching her head, I said, "Bibby, everything is going to be fine. We will talk about this tonight, but you have an obligation to go to practice." This is not the kind of soccer team where practice is optional if you're having a bad day.

She said, "I'm. Not. Going." While I recognized that look, I had never seen it before relative to soccer. In fact, I had never before seen Vivian get so knocked off her game. I was concerned, of course, but whether or not she was going, I was, because I had an obligation to get her teammate to practice.

I told Vivian, "You do what you want, but if you don't go to practice, you are letting them win. See ya." Then I walked downstairs.

I knew those were fighting words to Viv, so I was not surprised when minutes later I was in the car about to pull out of the garage when she came out of the door with her soccer bag, still crying. When she got in the car, I told her that I was proud of her. I still didn't know what happened, but it wasn't good, and she wasn't talking. I called Carey from the car in the few minutes we had before we picked up Mak (I knew Viv would *not* want us to talk about it in front of Mak). Carey didn't know any more than I did. By the time we got to Mak's house, which is only about five minutes away, to most people, Vivian looked as if nothing had happened. But I knew my daughter. I knew that focused, straight-ahead stare as if she were trying to will herself to think, feel, or do something.

Not a word was spoken on the way to practice. When I dropped them off, I waited until Mak was out of the car and Viv was about to close the door. I said, "Bibby, take it out on the ball. I love you."

She gave me just a twitch of a smile and a knowing nod and said, "I love you, too." And she was off.

Before putting the car back in drive, I said out loud to myself, "That's my Bibby."

I remember thinking, "I feel badly for anyone who goes up against her in practice today." But I knew the hard part for me was yet to come. In about two hours, Vivian would be dropped off at the house and I needed to be ready. But since all I really knew was that girls had been mean to her, it was going to have to be a cold read on my part. Neither Carey nor I had ever had to deal with Vivian's feelings relative to "mean girl" issues.

When Viv got home that night, she went straight for the kitchen to eat the dinner I had picked up for her. I said, "When you're done eating, can we talk?"

She said, "Sure," and that's just what we did.

A few girls who did not like Vivian's friendship with another girl were saying Vivian said something negative about that friend. For the purposes of this story, I'll call that friend Kate. Keep in mind that Kate is a wonderful little girl and a good friend to Vivian, as Vivian is to her. Also, you should rest assured that Carey and I are *not* the parents that defend our kids blindly. In fact, quite the opposite.

We always tell our kids that they should always first look at what portion of any problem they could have controlled. "Blame yourself first," we tell them, "even if you are only 2 percent of the problem." Identify that portion, take responsibility, and move on. There are many benefits to this. Obviously, it removes the other's argument against you and prevents them from assigning a disproportionate amount of blame to you through the general accusation of you having been wrong, too. But most importantly, it forces you to be self-reflective and evaluate the situation objectively—as it is, not as you wish it were. This level of reflection allows you to objectively review life outside of the Chaos Parallel. There is another benefit, as well. From my experience, one of the most predictive traits of a successful person is one who first seeks to take responsibility for their actions, as opposed to instinctively blaming others.

I reminded Vivian of this at the outset, but I could already tell she never said a word about Kate to these other kids. But just to be sure, as well as to get an updated baseline for my internal parental lie detector, I said, "Vivian, there are two people you don't lie to … ever … your doctor and your lawyer. Of course, you are going to lie to your parents on occasion, if you really want to get something (she laughed), but tonight I am your lawyer, so you need to tell me the truth."

She said, "I know that, Dad. But I didn't say anything. Why would I? I'm the one who defends Kate when other people make things up about her!"

As it turns out, Viv wasn't bothered at all by the three girls who said they hated her. She honestly didn't care; not in the overly defensive kind of way, but she sincerely was not troubled by that.

What bothered her deeply was that Kate, her friend, didn't believe her when she told Kate the rumor was untrue. Vivian said Kate started to ignore her and would not look at her. Viv told me that she tried several times, in several different ways, to assure Kate that the other girls were making stuff up, as usual. But Kate was having none of it.

Being shunned by her good friend seemed to compound the original problem of not being believed. This was the source of Vivian's pain. Now I understood it. I knew there was no way for me to fix her problem, and I told her as much. It would have to be worked out over time. But, as my dad did for me, I believed I could help her deal with it by helping her understand *why* Kate was reacting and behaving the way she was. I wanted to simply give my daughter a way to make sense of what she clearly saw as irrational and unfair behavior.

We talked for nearly two hours that night. I felt a little guilty, because I found myself almost glad that this had happened. It gave us a chance to talk—really talk—just the two of us. No TV, no phone, or iPad, not even Carey. Just us. It was great.

I first told Viv to stop trying to convince Kate of anything. It was obvious that doing so—and failing—was causing her even more stress. Being fully convinced that she was "innocent," I could move on with the "defense" of my daughter's peace of mind. I reminded her of what a buddy of mine, Jon Grimes, always says in situations where one has done nothing wrong. He says, "Don't explain. Don't complain." While being the first to admit it when you are at fault is a must, the opposite is equally important.

I told Vivian, as I had before, that when you are not at fault, never apologize for anything, or act even remotely contrite—not even to smooth things over. First of all, it is totally disingenuous, which immediately calls into question all of your previous and future sincere apologies. And secondly, it's insulting to the other person and cheapens the relationship. Anyone who needs to be placated is not your friend, or not one you should want. Finally, if you make a habit of this, the wrong type of person will actually learn to use it against you as relationship leverage. That leverage, in this context, is simply creating an insecurity in another person in such a way as to lead them to seek you out. People who do this wish to create a power dynamic as a way of controlling the relationship, or worse, you.

Yes, if you're wondering, this is exactly what I talked to Vivian about. I made sure to tell her that Kate, in all likelihood, was not doing any of this intentionally. However, if Vivian continued to chase Kate around trying to convince her of something she should believe anyway—based on years of friendship—the result would be the same. It would be the basis of an unhealthy relationship that would forever bounce in and out of the Chaos Parallel. I wanted Vivian to know that some people almost instinctively seek to create insecurities in others as both a shield and a sword. While some adults I know have made it an art form, you see kids do it to each other all the time through their cliques and groups and strength-in-numbers bit. And given their fragile psyches, often with great success.

Creating an insecurity in another is all about instilling doubt, just as having an insecurity is all about accepting that doubt that some aspect of who we are does not measure up to something or someone else.

Regardless of age, creating an insecurity in another is all about instilling doubt, just as having an insecurity is all about accepting that doubt that some aspect of who we are does not measure up to something or someone else. The questioning of who we are can have deleterious effects on our thoughts, feelings, decisions, and relationships—most importantly, the one we have with ourselves. We see it play out every day in every aspect of our lives, from the totally benign to the catastrophic.

Something as simple as telling someone they look tired when they first get to work can take their mind off their daily tasks by shifting their focus from what they need to do, to what others think of them. Obviously, the opposite is true. It's why we like compliments so much. When someone tells us they like our haircut, or dress, or smile, we feel good—more confident. Our haircut, dress, or smile would not have been any different had we not received the compliment; it only served as confirmation that some aspect of us was acceptable in the eyes of someone else. Any doubt we carry with us about ourselves can often be removed, or significantly diminished, with just a few positive words from others. Unfortunately, and all too often, the words of others can negatively alter the perception we have of ourselves, and even cause us to question what we believe or know to be true.

Yesterday, I was talking to my real estate agent, Harry, since my wife and I are looking for some property. We found a tract of land that we were willing to pay X for, because that is what we believed it to be worth and were willing to pay. As soon as Harry told me that the owner didn't want to sell, I immediately wanted it more and was willing to pay X+ for it. It was insane. Fortunately, I caught myself and we are moving on. But that experience reminded me of something my dad always used to tell me, relative to any negotiation. He said that the best time to buy a house or car is when you don't need one. While the concept is a little odd, since we don't usually buy things that significant if we don't need them, it is, nevertheless, true. But why? Because even something as simple as need and desire is correctly seen as weakness, just as a lack of need or desire is perceived as strength. Both contribute to the formation of a power structure, or at least attempt to. Why do you suppose people are so quick to exclaim, "I don't care"? Because it's simply a common, reflexive defense to prove their lack of vulnerability and cover up insecurity they have about the topic or their position.

I remember Carey coming home from work years ago and asking me how I would handle a situation with one of her coworkers—let's call her Laura. Laura was perpetually rude and dismissive of Carey. Carey sounded off to me for about ten straight minutes and then concluded with, "You know what, I don't even care what she thinks." I smiled and went in for a condescending hug. Carey just *loves* it when I do that. Of course, I ended up telling her what I would do, which totally worked, by the way. But I couldn't help myself: I had to first address her meager attempt to convince herself she could not be hurt. I told Carey to think of something that she truly, actually, and totally did *not* care about. Then I asked her to think of the last time she ever told anybody about it. Never, because she *actually* didn't care. The only thing you know when someone tells you they don't care is that they do—the question is how much. It is a telltale sign that there is at least a trace of insecurity in them about that topic.

For whatever it's worth, here was my advice to Carey: I told her to stop acknowledging Laura's existence, even if they were the only two on an elevator and it was uncomfortable. I told Carey to imagine that she (Carey) was the only person in the room—to act, think, and move as if this were the case. Further, since they worked together, I said that if she had to interact with Laura, she should not look Laura in the eye, but instead, stare just above her eyes, or hairline. Less than a week later, Carey came home, tossed her keys on the kitchen island, and started to laugh as she said, "Well, guess who wants to be my

BFF now?" I didn't even answer her obviously rhetorical question. I just laughed and went in for another condescending hug.

See, Laura probably never disliked Carey, she just disliked the parts of herself that Carey reminded her of every time she looked at Carey. And the fact that there isn't a scintilla of Carey's being that even seems to be aware of her qualities bothered Laura even more. Further, Laura's sudden interest and friendliness toward Carey had nothing to do with her liking Carey. It had everything to do with Laura simply not wanting to be disliked or ignored by Carey. The doubt she sought to instill in Carey had now been flipped back on her. All Carey had to do was spend three days creating an insecurity in Laura in order to change her behavior. While Carey did care, I don't believe it was about wanting to be friends with Laura, thus the sword; but rather, she was far more interested in Laura simply not being rude to her, thus the shield.

Knowing that I didn't want to corrupt my child just to help her deal with Kate, I chose to make my point to Vivian using an example to which she could relate. Since our backyard is not very big—at least not for five active dogs—we take them and the kids to the dog park pretty regularly for exercise and to get them to calm down (it helps the dogs, too). I told Vivian to imagine that we were at the dog park and she were right next to a dog she had never met before. I asked her what would happen if she started running toward that dog. "It would run away," she said. Right. But then I asked her what would happen if, instead of running toward the dog, she ran away from it. What would it do then? "Chase me," she said. Right again. So, how can that be explained logically?

Running from something usually indicates a desire to get away from it, just as running after something usually indicates a desire to get closer to it. "So, why would the same dog, under the same conditions, want to chase you when it just wanted to get away from you?" I asked.

"I don't know; that's weird," she said.

I told her that while it may seem "weird," it was actually quite normal. In fact, it is sort of a base-level instinct built inside of all of us. We pursue that which retreats. Things that move away from us possess an inherent quality, or at least the perception of one. That is, they seemingly possess something of value, something we should want or desire, maybe something rare or unattainable, or perhaps even something that we are not worthy of possessing—thus we pursue it.

In the 2000 movie *The Tao of Steve*, from where that phrase originated, the phrase "We pursue that which retreats from us," is used to explain one of the three "rules" for landing an otherwise unattainable object of one's affection.[4] The rules themselves purport to be Ladies' Man 101 knowledge. In short, they are as follows:

1. **Be Desireless.** In this context, it does not mean that one should not be desired, nor does it mean that one should *pretend* to not desire; it means that one should *actually* let go of one's desires.

2. **Be Excellent.** While not relevant to the concepts in this chapter, you've come this far with me, so it would be a shame not to include it. It essentially means one must do something great in the presence of the other.

3. **Be Gone.** While pretty self-explanatory, it is the basis of the aforementioned phrase, and sadly, it's pure genius, albeit totally manipulative.

---

4   Duncan North, Greer Goodman, and Jenniphr Goodman, *The Tao of Steve*, directed by Jenniphr Goodman, Los Angeles, CA: Sony Pictures Classics, Inc., 2000.

Of course, while it makes for a great story line in a movie about hooking up with those otherwise out of one's league, it is not the thing of which actual, meaningful relationships are made. So, I was walking a fine line with my then eleven-year-old daughter. On the one hand, I wanted her to be aware of the concept that was perhaps being used against her as a sword, even if done so instinctively, not as the result of malice on the part of Kate. On the other hand, I didn't want to teach or encourage her to manipulate others, which honestly is pretty easy to do, especially to other kids. My fundamental belief in Vivian's goodness gave me great confidence that she was more likely to use the information to make sense of the behavior of others, rather than to take advantage of them.

It was nearly 10:30 p.m. as we wrapped up our conversation. It was well past Vivian's bedtime, but Carey wasn't home to break up the party. Even if she had been, she is usually dead asleep by 9:00 p.m. and probably doesn't know that Vivian literally never goes to bed on time. A combination of being a night owl myself, learning to pick my battles with Vivian, and the fact that staying up late does not seem to negatively affect a single aspect of her life, I usually just let her go to bed whenever she wants. But unlike other nights, when we would both be watching two different TVs in two different rooms on two different floors—that night was different. We were together—talking, growing, and learning together.

As Viv un-propped her legs and pulled back the blanket she had been using as the last line of defense against the subarctic temperature Carey keeps our house at, she shifted her tiny frame toward the edge, signaling she had enough. Vivian let out a sigh, which I've learned from Carey, who does the same thing, indicates the end of a conversation or that she desperately just wants to go to bed at the end of the evening—usually about the same time my brain is starting to function. But, unlike Carey, Vivian didn't get up, give me a kiss, and disappear into our bedroom. She stayed. While Vivian's sigh was, in fact, the end of the conversation, it wasn't that she wanted to leave. It was something else entirely. When I looked at her just sitting there on the couch—her feet still not touching the ground beneath her—I saw a peace, a softness, a rare look of contentment coming from my otherwise uber-focused daughter. I smiled and said, "You're okay, aren't you?"

She said, "Yep."

I said again, as I often do, "That's my Bibby."

So, if you know a Vivian, I suppose my encouragement would be this: Good luck. Or, you could do what I do—just get out of the way, and even if you have to move mountains to do so, make sure to be there for those precious, fortuitous moments when she actually *needs* you. Believe me, when someone like Vivian needs you—and you are actually able to help her—it will make you feel like you've swallowed sunshine.

CHAPTER EIGHTEEN

BEN

I t was the morning of August 11, 1995. I was a junior at TCU and living in whatever apartment complex was foolish enough to lease to college students with a destructive, barking dog named Nick. The phone rang. Despite being mid-shower, I stepped out to answer it. Since there were no cell phones, phone calls were a mildly important event in my life. While most of the calls I received were ultimately unremarkable, this call was actually important, and the news it conveyed drastically changed the landscape of my life.

Growing up, my siblings and I were required to answer the phone, "Hello, this is (insert name)." So, when I lived on my own, I instituted my own rebellious method of answering the phone. "Yeah," I said. On the other end was a friend of mine. "Alex, this is Brad. How are you, man?"

"Wet," I responded. Then he said it. "Hey, man, did you hear about Ben's parents?"

This world doesn't seem to comprehend the true meaning of the word friendship—nearly mocking its existence with the ubiquitous moniker "BFF"—the application of which can change with not so much as an eye roll. If you are able to go through life with one—just one—amazing, true, trustworthy friend, count yourself fortunate; you are blessed.

As for me, I don't have many friends—at least not the way I think of it. There are dozens—perhaps hundreds—of people with whom I am friendly or enjoy spending time. I do not intend to devalue their contribution to my life; all have been significant, and some profoundly impactful. However, there may only be three people outside of my family who are constants. They are simply irreplaceable, woven tightly into the fabric of my being. They are there even when they're not. They are part of who and why I am.

Even among those select few in my life, there is a shining star. A go-to. A ride-or-die guy. Like family, only maybe a little better since he was not given to me, but rather chosen. With friends, unlike family, the eye-roll exit is always an option. But with true friends—special ones—that exit isn't reflexively taken. In fact, lifelong friends are not merely chosen, they are re-chosen and re-chosen—constantly making the cut, regardless of the challenges and tests that life and relationships hand them. Further, lifelong friendships don't simply weather storms and emerge on the other side clinging to the status quo. A hallmark of true friendship is that both friends grow and learn from those experiences. Those moments are periodic springboards to the next meaningful level of reliance, trust, and love.

For the last quarter century, Ben has been that friend for me. Like most friends, we've lived, traveled, and worked together. We've competed with and against each other in just about every sport there is. We've been kicked out of bars and were, of course, the best men in each other's weddings. We are always present for the births of each other's children, we take nearly every vacation together, and we spend every Thanksgiving and Christmas as families. To really drive home the point, after my wife, kids, and dad, Ben is the next "favorite" on my phone. Now that's status.

I mentioned earlier that friends like Ben are there even when they're not. At times, they are also there when *you're* not. Like the time Carey wanted to take a hip-hop dance class. It was our first year of marriage and I didn't yet realize I was obligated to do things that I didn't want to do. After I absolutely refused to take the class with her, Carey's next call was to Ben. He said yes. Of course, he kind of had to since Carey agreed to let Ben live with us for the first year of our marriage.

You read that correctly. After law school, I had planned to move back to Fort Worth and get a house with Ben. Well, I met and married Carey. Having never been married before, I failed to see why this new wrinkle should change the plans I had with Ben. Carey didn't get it at first, but she was a quick study. She could see that Ben and I were a package deal.

My first memory of Ben came during an intramural football game in college. Our initial interaction came even before the opening kickoff. We got into a fight with each other. In and of itself, a couple of college kids getting into a sports fight isn't a shocking headline. What made it noteworthy is that we were on the same team. In any event, we both thought—knew, actually—that we, not the other, should be the one to return the opening kickoff. When it came time to take the field, neither of us relented. We tried to occupy the same space on the field, and it didn't work out. To this day, I don't remember who ultimately returned that kickoff, but if we didn't score, it was probably Ben.

Before that game, I'd seen Ben maybe a handful of times, as we had some mutual friends. After that game, although we continued to play on the same intramural teams for years, we didn't intentionally hang out much. I didn't like him and I'm pretty sure he didn't like me—a far cry from where we are twenty-five years later. So, how did it happen? Why? Like I stated before, that phone call from Brad changed the landscape of my life, but it shattered Ben's.

Having not bothered to find a towel before answering the phone, I stood motionless when Brad asked me if I had heard about Ben's parents. "No. What happened?" I asked, of course. Despite my feelings toward Ben at the time, Brad's answer devastated me. I couldn't imagine. No one could.

Now, keep in mind that Ben is very important to me now and generally a private person, so it is with gentle fingers that I type this story. For years and years, people—including my own kids—have asked me, "What happened to Ben's parents?" My answer has always been the same.

"It's not my story to tell," I would say.

Well, it is still Ben's. So, it is with his permission that I share what is a necessary backdrop to a far more important question, "What happened to Ben?" That story *is* mine to tell, and the answer changed my life. It is my hope it will have an impact on yours, as well.

That story is mine to tell, and the answer changed my life.

Ben is the only child of Renee and Robert. They spent Ben's early years in New Jersey before his family moved to Houston, Texas, when Ben was nine years old. He had a normal childhood with ups and downs and everything in between, as many of us had. He remembers his parents being happy and extremely trusting of him.

His parents were the furthest thing from the "helicopter" parents we see today. Ben was given a tremendous amount of freedom, a symbol of his parents' faith and trust in Ben and his ability to take care of himself. In hindsight, Ben is now thankful for the inadvertent gift he was given to rely on himself as a child. He would eventually need every bit of those experiences and independence.

After visiting several different schools with his mom and dad, Ben enrolled at TCU in Fort Worth following his high school graduation. His first few years in college brought the usual visits back to Houston to spend holidays, breaks, and long weekends with his parents. Sometime before his junior year in college, unbeknownst to Ben, his dad informed his mom that he wanted a separation.

Bob and Renee ultimately separated in December of 1994, however, they didn't tell their son until May of 1995. In fact, a month before he found out, Ben had been home for Easter and saw no signs of discord. Bob actually moved back in the house for the weekend, and as Ben now puts it, "acted" like everything was fine.

Soon thereafter, Bob began showing noticeable signs of change to his personality, his attitude, and even his physical appearance. Despite the fact that it was Bob's idea to separate—not Renee's—it took a significant toll on him. Bob was always a bigger guy—around 240 pounds. By August of that same year, he was down to 185 pounds. Bob began acting and saying things that seemed unreal to Ben, untethered to anything he had experienced or witnessed as a child. During this time, Bob drove up to Fort Worth to take Ben to a Texas Rangers baseball game. It was there—as they sat in their seats—that Bob told his son that he was going to kill his mom and himself.

Whatever you think you would have done or thought or said in that moment, unless you've been there, don't. There isn't a playbook or how-to manual for that. Let's just say, Ben did everything a twenty-year-old living three hundred miles away could have done under those circumstances. Unimaginable.

Months later, on August 9, 1995, Ben's dad drove to his mom's house with a gun and did what he said he was going to do. Ben's mom had been trying to move forward with her life after the separation and had begun dating someone. Unfortunately, that man's life was also taken that day. As if the utter shock of these events were not enough, Ben would also learn that his dad's attempt to end his life was not immediately successful.

As next of kin, and technically an adult, Ben would be tasked with making a horrific decision. After three weeks of dealing with media, attorneys, and hospital personnel, not to mention getting all manner of his parents' affairs in order and planning and attending his mom's funeral in New Jersey, Ben signed the paperwork to have his father removed from life support.

I asked Ben if he ever wished his dad had survived. He responded with an emphatic, "Never. Not once." However, he went on to tell me, "But you want to know what's weird? Even though I knew it was coming—I had already signed the paperwork—when I actually got the call that he was gone, I collapsed on my bed and bawled my eyes out just repeating 'I'm all alone now! I'm all alone now!' That's when it hit me."

I have three moms, two dads, two sisters, a brother, a wife, three kids, and a treasure trove of coping mechanisms that I've accumulated over forty-five years of life. For twenty-five years, I have considered these events. For a year and a half, I have known I would get to this point in the book and have to begin writing about it, and I am having difficulty.

Ben was twenty years old. No brothers. No sisters. No parents. Most importantly, this was happening to *him*. What must the world have looked like for *Ben* in that moment? I have talked to Ben at least fifty times about the events of that day and of those that both preceded and followed them. In fact, after ten years of friendship, I started to notice a trend. Ben would go an entire year without saying a word about it. Then, as if on cue, we would find ourselves in a deep, meaningful, and always difficult conversation. Each year revealed another facet of what Ben had been through, who he was, how he handled it, the effect it had on his life, and what gave him the strength to move forward. I know the phrase tends to get overused, but really getting to know Ben has been like peeling back an onion, one layer at a time.

So, how did Ben and I go from fighting on a football field to being inextricable parts of each other's lives? Well, like most things in my life, I believe it was providential. After that phone call from Brad, who was one of our mutual-but-separate friends, I didn't see or talk to Ben for over six months—no one did. We later found out that he spent the first few weeks in Houston, then a couple of weeks with his mom's family in New Jersey before returning to Houston to live with his dad's brother, Uncle Rich—great guy, by the way. Ben once told me, "I won't ever be able to repay Rich for what he did for me." I know Uncle Rich, and I can assure you, he doesn't require repayment.

Needless to say, Ben didn't return to TCU that semester—there were still too many family matters with which to deal. When he wasn't handling estates or managing the emotional chasm that now permanently existed between the families, Ben was a substitute teacher in the Houston public school system. I would have paid top dollar to watch that unfold, as one of the lovely traits Ben and I share is a lack of patience.

Then one day, a bunch of us were playing roller hockey on the tennis courts of our apartment complex. Out of the clear blue, Ben showed up. It wasn't the reunion you might have expected. No one ran over to him and gave him a hug. I'm not sure the game even completely stopped. I don't think anyone really knew what to say. It was weird.

About a week earlier, my girlfriend and I were randomly talking about how people like to be treated after losing a loved one. She was taking a child psychology class and was simply telling me about it. She said that people don't want to be ignored as if they have leprosy, but all too often they are, mostly because others are unsure about what to say, how to say it, or if the grieving person even wants their loss acknowledged. Well, according to her, they do. Ben was the furthest thing from my mind when she was explaining this a week earlier, but it was all I could think about when I saw him standing against the fence by himself. I stopped playing and skated over to him. I asked him how and what he was doing. Where had he been? Was he coming back to school? Somewhat surprisingly, I don't remember much about that conversation—and I tend to remember most conversations. What sticks out to me is that I was drawn to him. Five minutes before he walked up to that court is the last time I can remember my life without Ben.

Now, as with all of life, there are some realities. Here are a few:

Ben is no saint—at least he didn't use to be. He is also no picnic to be around when he's pissed, which actually doesn't happen that much anymore, but it used to.

He is perpetually late to everything—a personal pet peeve of mine. Worse, he will more often than not lie about where he is and how long it will take him to get to where he was supposed to be fifteen minutes earlier. When we are scheduled to meet for lunch and he isn't there on time, I'll give him a call. He will invariably say, "I'm five minutes away." I now know that means he is leaving his office, which is usually twenty minutes away.

He doesn't take other people's point of view into consideration as often as I'd like or think he should, and he almost never apologizes for anything.

Oh, and I almost forgot: he isn't particularly funny—unless he is trying to tell a joke after a few too many glasses of wine, in which case everyone is pretty much just laughing *at* him. I could go on, but you get the point: Ben is human.

Although his faults were far more serious than bad joke telling or being late, Ben's dad was human, as well. In his final act of humanity, mired in despair, Bob left a note.

"It wasn't so much a note," Ben told me, "it was more like a novel."

Bob had written a letter detailing everything about his life, right to the very end. In it, he described his own childhood, along with his years of marriage to Renee, as "idyllic." He addressed everyone in the family and then some. He wrote quite a bit directly to his son, Ben. Despite the detail and length, Ben has only read the letter once in all these years. He told me that he only remembers one thing about the entire letter.

"He wrote that I would be fine. That I was resilient and that I would bounce back from this," Ben once told me. As misapplied as it might be, how's *that* for trust and faith in one's son? While I've never told Ben this, I've always found it interesting that of all the thoughts his dad expressed to him in that letter, *that* is the part he remembers. I gotta say, as cold as it seems, he wasn't wrong.

However, there's "fine" and then there's "functional." Ben had to conquer the latter before he could work toward the former. And it wasn't so much a "bounce" as it was a painful, grueling, treacherous struggle for Ben to pick up the pieces of his shattered life. The comfort and security of the small but loving nuclear family he had once known had been taken from him in an instant. Aside from the painfully obvious ramifications, there were also subtler but altogether real and lasting consequences of the trauma he endured. While Ben never lost his well-displayed self-confidence, as we all got older, that which seemed perfectly normal years before began looking a little different. Eventually, Carey and I got it, but it took a while.

Ben had actually been on the first nondate date that Carey and I ever went on. After I graduated from law school, I spent an extra week in Tulsa to take a victory lap with my friends before moving back to Texas and having to deal with real life. Ben bought a one-way ticket to help me pack up my things and drive my car back to Fort Worth, with my U-Haul van in tow. The girl I was dating at the time, Sara, had actually gone with me to pick up Ben at the airport. Graciously, she saw that I wanted to spend the last night packing with Ben and told me that she was going to visit her parents in Oklahoma City and that she would see me in a week when she came down to visit. I said goodbye to her, then Ben and I went to pick up the U-Haul. As we pulled up to my house, I turned to Ben and said, "Hey, man. I don't want you to think badly of me, but there is this girl who I used to clerk for, and I can't leave town without at least trying to call her. I swear, I'm just gonna try her. If she doesn't answer, I'm sure I'll never talk to her again." Those were my exact words. Ben looked at me and started laughing. He didn't know Sara from a hole in the wall and certainly didn't care that I wanted to call some other girl who probably didn't remember who I was. He said, "Dude, do whatever you want. Just see if she has a friend."

I called the only number I had for my former boss, Carey. It had been a couple of months since I worked for her, and law clerks come and go, so I really didn't know what to expect in the off-chance she did answer the phone. To my surprise, not only was she home, she *did* remember me, although she was audibly surprised to hear from me.

She said, "What's wrong, didn't they let you graduate?" I suppose she suspected I approached school like I approached my clerkship with her—which was basically that I kind of did things by my own rules. I told her that they had, in fact, tried to keep me from graduating, but that I had naked pictures of the dean, so everything worked out. I'm not sure if she knew I was kidding.

I told her that the reason I was calling was to see if she wanted to meet some friends and me for drinks at a bar near her house (I wanted to make it as hard as possible for her to say no). To my further surprise, she said yes. I forgot to ask about the friend for Ben, but Carey brought one anyway. We drank and talked and laughed until 2:00 a.m., and then moved the party to my front porch and perhaps other parts of the house.

Carey told me it was a good thing Cheryl was there or else she never would have gone with me. Whatever. Carey and I wound up talking until 6:00 a.m. At one point, the noise from Ben and Cheryl in the other room stopped. Then we heard my car start and drive off. Carey and I looked at each other and started laughing. To this day, I don't know where they went, but if I never said it, buddy, thanks. Good looking out.

That night was May 13, 2000. Carey and I got engaged on September 13, 2000. On the day of our wedding, Ben turned to me and said, "Man, you remember when we dropped them off at Carey's house at 6:30 that morning?" Knowing exactly what was coming next,

I said, "I know … I know."

He said, "I *never* thought we would see either one of them again. But here we are. You did it."

I had done it. I had gotten married. After living with Carey and me for a year, Ben started to take the hint. He had a good job and reluctantly got an apartment—not a house, an apartment. Life went on and Carey and I started having kids. Ben, who is tall, dark, and apparently handsome, had a series of girlfriends, some of whom he really liked. But each one had an expiration date, as Carey likes to say. After a while, Carey started grilling him about when he was going to settle down … maybe get a dog, a house, something. Ben would blow it off and we didn't think much of it.

After a few years, with our second son on the way, Carey and I moved out of the house we had lived in since getting married. We knew Ben didn't like change and the only chance of getting him to commit to a house would be if it were someplace familiar. Since Ben knew the house well, we finally convinced him to buy ours. After living there for well over a year, he still had just the one chair sitting in front of a TV on a stand in the family room. He had shelves of baseball trophies where you would expect a man of his age to have pictures and clocks. This bothered Carey, but not for the reasons it bothered me. This had been Carey's house and she couldn't stand to see it unfurnished. As time marched on, I saw something missing in my friend's life, but it wasn't a clock.

In fairness, Ben has always been a minimalist—the polar opposite of me—but it was getting a little weird. I finally said to him, "Bud, why don't you at least buy a rug?"

"I don't need one," he would say.

"How about a couch?" I'd ask.

"I've looked, but can't decide on one I really like," he'd say.

"Okay, well at least get a bed frame so your mattress doesn't sit on the floor," I'd encourage him.

"Why?" he'd ask.

Good question.

The better question was, why wouldn't Ben commit to anything? Not a long-term relationship. Not a dog, or a rug, or a couch, or even a bed frame. As much as I loved Ben, I knew I was a poor substitute for a professional who actually knew how to help him. I knew Ben needed to really talk and get some things out. I didn't think our talks, while meaningful, were really moving the needle. He needed to recognize and understand first what was going on, and eventually why. He needed to learn how to overcome the life-altering effects of what the Chaos Parallel did to his life.

I reached out to a doctor friend of mine who knew Ben well. Knowing that Ben is a private person and that Fort Worth can be a "small town" when it comes to news, I asked for the name of someone in Dallas. I sat down with Ben one day and said that I thought he needed to talk to someone. I told him I had the name of a highly recommended professional. I assured him that I was all in and that I would go with him to every session. He was appreciative of the effort and wasn't as resistant to the idea as I thought he might be. In the end, we never went together. To this day, I actually don't even know if Ben ever sought professional counseling, but if he did, he never told me about it.

What I do know is that Ben and I never stopped talking and we eventually did talk about his lack of commitment. More specifically, we've discussed, many times, how the experience with his parents created an understandable fear of change and loss. But this wasn't your garden-variety loss. It wasn't even just the traumatic loss it appeared to be, on its face. It was all-encompassing. Ben once told Carey that he didn't just lose his parents; he lost everything. He lost his future with them.

Without any brothers or sisters, he lost the link to his past, through stories and lessons that would never again be told. He realized he would never again get a birthday present from them, or a card, or a phone call. His last sit-down dinner with them was now behind him. Where would he go for holidays? There was no "home." From a practical standpoint, he lost the typical financial support afforded to most kids in college, or at least the parental safety net. He wasn't even talking about big things like tuition, a place to live, or transportation, although many kids have their parents partial contribution to at least one or two of those. Ben would never again get to ask, "Can I borrow the gas card?" or "Can you spare a twenty?" Imagine going from having a family one day to not even having health insurance the next. I don't care how much freedom you were given as a child—nothing prepares you for that kind of independence.

For Ben, having or relying on anything meant it could be taken away. This ran deep, even with little things. Ben and I have been skiing together a million times. His lips get disgustingly chapped every time, but he refuses to use lip balm, saying, "I don't need it" every time I offer. This happened for years—literally. I finally asked him why the hell he wouldn't just use lip balm. He told me that once he used it, then he would need it. Then if he didn't have it, it would piss him off.

What? Okay, that actually made sense, after I thought about it.

I told him that he was right and that I was pissed when I couldn't find mine. However, I get around that problem by simply carrying about ten of them with me at all times and having them stashed in every conceivable nook and cranny of my drawers, cars, pockets, etc. While true in my case, this was clearly not the point. If Ben didn't have anything, he couldn't lose anything. After the truck he had when his parents passed away stopped running, he rented a car for an entire year claiming he just couldn't decide what to buy. Imagine that.

This is why I admire Ben so much. He lost his parents, his entire understanding of what his intended life was meant to be, and inherited an insecurity that he had no hand in creating.

What's more impressive is that he eventually recognized it and admitted to me—but most importantly, to himself—where it came from and how it affected his life. Ben's insecurity about loss was significant, and eventually obvious to those around him. It might be a stretch to label his insecurity debilitating, but it was certainly not a phase or something that would pass on its own. Ben had to wrestle with and fight his insecurity every day. It wasn't a mere preference or strong discomfort like one might have about not taking their shirt off in public. This was not in his head—it had been shoved down his throat, against his will, by life. Ben had to work at it every day—against everything that was remotely comfortable. He had to be intentional about confronting his fears and moving forward despite them. Maybe we all should.

Like with most insecurities—especially those that are not self-inflicted—we don't tend to "fix" or

> **He had to be intentional about confronting his fears and moving forward despite them. Maybe we all should.**

"get over" them; they are always with us and apart of who we are. However, if we are honest with ourselves, we can recognize them, understand them, and seek to find a way to live our most authentic lives free from the chaos they often create. Ben did this.

Almost twelve years ago, Ben started to make some changes. He bought a new car. He was accepted into TCU's business school and attended classes at night while working full time as an executive. After three years, he graduated with his MBA. He not only bought a bed, he got end tables, lamps, rugs, and yes, a couch. And he even hung pictures and had a guest room. And get this, he painted the entire interior of the house, although Carey didn't approve of the color. It didn't matter. We were both happy for him—proud of him, actually.

Ben's progress—symbolized by evidence of permanence in and around his house and life—was not in overcoming his fear of commitment, which was rooted in his fear of loss. It was having the perseverance to continue living in spite of it. But Carey wanted more. She wanted the girl, the kiddos, the whole nine yards. She loves Ben, but it was now time for Ben to return the favor. In Carey's mind, it was his turn to supply the friend. Baby steps.

Knowing Ben has been a blessing and a curse in one regard. As it relates to my tolerance for other people's complaints about their lot in life, due to what they consider to be forces that act against them, I have little sympathy. Ben has set the victim benchmark so high I doubt blind, starving kittens would qualify. If anyone could ever bitch about their circumstances, Ben could. Despite the easy out, he never has.

You might recall in an earlier chapter I wrote about one of the most telling predictors of a successful person being that they first seek to take responsibility for themselves and don't tend to blame others. Ben embodied this, even when the world would have understood if he hadn't. With this defining character trait, we all knew Ben would eventually "bounce back," but he wasn't there yet.

In addition to just caring about my friend and wanting to help him work through things in whatever small way I could, my insatiable desire to know what motivates people had to know how he managed. How could someone who had been through so much be so, I don't know … *normal?* I know people to this day who still blame all their problems on the fact that their parents took their "blankie" away from them as a child. As mentioned, Ben doesn't blame anyone for anything. Why the hell not? I mean, buddy, you're sitting on a get-out-of-jail-free card. Aren't you *ever* gonna use it?

Well, as I've learned, Ben isn't "normal" at all, in this regard. He is exceptional. If this had been me, I would have started every business presentation with, "Hey, just want to let you know what I've been through, so in case I don't make any sense, that's why." I might even have signs or cards made. I would hand them out to people to help them "put me in context." Never any of that with Ben.

So, one day, during one of our annual talks, I asked him how and why. How did he get through it? Why didn't he make excuses? His answer—not just what he said, but also how he said it—remains the single most impactful thing he has ever said to me. It also made me a perpetually undesirable mark for would-be sympathy seekers.

This particular conversation took place in his driveway about ten years into our friendship. As mentioned, these were unplanned annual talks—they just sort of happened that way, as if he needed to get it out once a year. That afternoon I had driven him home from someplace and we had been casually talking about his childhood. When I pulled into his driveway, he didn't get out; he just kept talking. That was my cue to put the car in park and talk as long as he wanted. He started to cry, which he had done a few times before, but only in the preceding few years. But this time was a bit different. There was a little anger mixed with the sadness.

Our conversations to this point had mostly centered on his mom and him. His dad was only a fact character in our talks, not an emotional one. I had seen Ben angry many, many times, but never before while talking about his mom and dad. At an appropriate lull, I said, "Bud, I gotta ask you something. As you know, I have people in my family who walk around blaming everything and everyone for every aspect of their lives. They attribute their present circumstances to events and actions of others that happened decades ago. They tell themselves how this or that isn't fair. How are you walking around and why don't you ever complain about it?"

Ben paused, let out a sigh, then dropped his head allowing his chin to touch his chest. He stayed like that for just a few seconds, then popped his head back up and looked right at me. He got that same half-angry, half-focused look that he always got when someone had pissed him off just enough to make him want to beat them in any game we were playing, but not so angry that he lost all focus and ability to do so. Half shouting, he said, "You wanna know why? I'll tell you why. I got dealt a shitty hand in life. The way I see it, I can either fold or play." With each word becoming louder and more intense, he picked up his right hand, stretched it out flat, and while slamming his hand on the top of my dashboard, he said, "I'm fuckin' playing!"

Never. Never before had I heard Ben talk like that in relation to this topic—or any topic, for that matter. First, Ben is not foul-mouthed—far from it. It just came out that way and I did not see the point in editing his words. That's what he said—verbatim. Either I had never asked the right question, or he wasn't ready to give it. As I look back, I think it is possible that he himself had only recently discovered his voice, although I've never asked him.

Carey eventually got her wish; Ben finally returned the favor and brought a friend to our three-person party, and she was perfect in every way for him. On March 21, 2015, at the age of forty, my buddy got married to the most amazing girl he could ever ask for. Ben and Emily, or Bemily, as they're known in some circles, now have three impossibly cute kids—Leighton Renee, Brooks Benjamin, and Beckett Munson.

Despite Emily's desire to get a bigger place, they still live in the same house, of course. Probably sensing she should settle in, Emily did completely redecorate the interior and it looks amazing. Carey loves the paint color, so we can all rest easy. My brother, Carey, and I are constantly working on Emily's behalf by sending Ben listings of new homes and dragging him to open houses hoping someday he will cave. However, their house is the only one Ben has ever lived in during his twenty-seven years in Fort Worth, so good luck getting him to move. Baby steps …

The reason "Ben" is the last chapter in this book, as I always knew it would be, is because his story, in many ways, is *not* unlike everyone else's. Of course, his is a magnified version on steroids, but the concepts are the same. Ben's words in my car that day still resonate not just because of what they meant in the context of his circumstances, but because of what they mean to all of us. We can't control everything that happens to or around us. We oftentimes can't even control the impact events can have—if only temporary—on our lives, our thoughts, our feelings, or our relationships. We can't always predict how our past circumstances and experiences might affect how we view the world or the insecurities they might create in us.

However, we can choose to recognize those moments, those events, and those experiences for what they are and the impact they have on our lives. We can choose to see the world for what it is, not as we wish it were or the way it could have been if only …

And we can choose to view our reality as opportunity rather than viewing it as a helpless victim would.

We can be both aware of our insecurities *and* be unable to change them—yet *still* manage to make sense of them and move forward. We get there by asking why and telling ourselves the truth about whatever the answer actually is. When life gets hard, unmanageable, even seemingly hopeless—don't cash in your chips.

Don't fold. Think of Ben.

Keep playing.